W9-BAT-461

THE CHEESEMONGER'S SEASONS

THE
CHEESEMONGER'S SEASONS

Recipes for
Enjoying
Cheeses with
Ripe Fruits
and Vegetables

CHESTER HASTINGS

FOREWORD BY
CLIFFORD A. WRIGHT

PHOTOGRAPHS BY
JOSEPH DE LEO AND CHESTER HASTINGS

CHRONICLE BOOKS
SAN FRANCISCO

Library of Congress Cataloging-in-Publication Data
available.

ISBN 978-1-4521-1288-6

Manufactured in China

MIX
Paper from
responsible sources
FSC
www.fsc.org
FSC® C008047

Design by VANESSA DINA
Food styling by CHRISTINE ALBANO
Prop styling by LUCY ATTWATER

Joseph De Leo wishes to thank his crew, Kaz, Christine,
Lucy, and Nora, for their incredible talents and enthusiasm.

Thank you also to Chester Hastings and Vanessa Dina for
allowing me to work on another beautiful project, and to
ABC Carpet and Home, Murray's Cheeses, and Melissa's
Produce for your contributions.

Photographs on pages 19, 20, 25, 31, 35, 53, 57, 73, 79,
83, 105, 109, 127, 133, 137, 150, 157, 158, 161, 165, 171,
and 173 by Chester Hastings.

Excerpt on page 90 from The Snack Thief by Andrea
Camilleri, translated by Stephen Sartarelli, and published
in 2004 by Penguin Group (USA).

10 9 8 7 6 5 4 3 2

Chronicle Books LLC
680 Second Street
San Francisco, California 94107
WWW.CHRONICLEBOOKS.COM

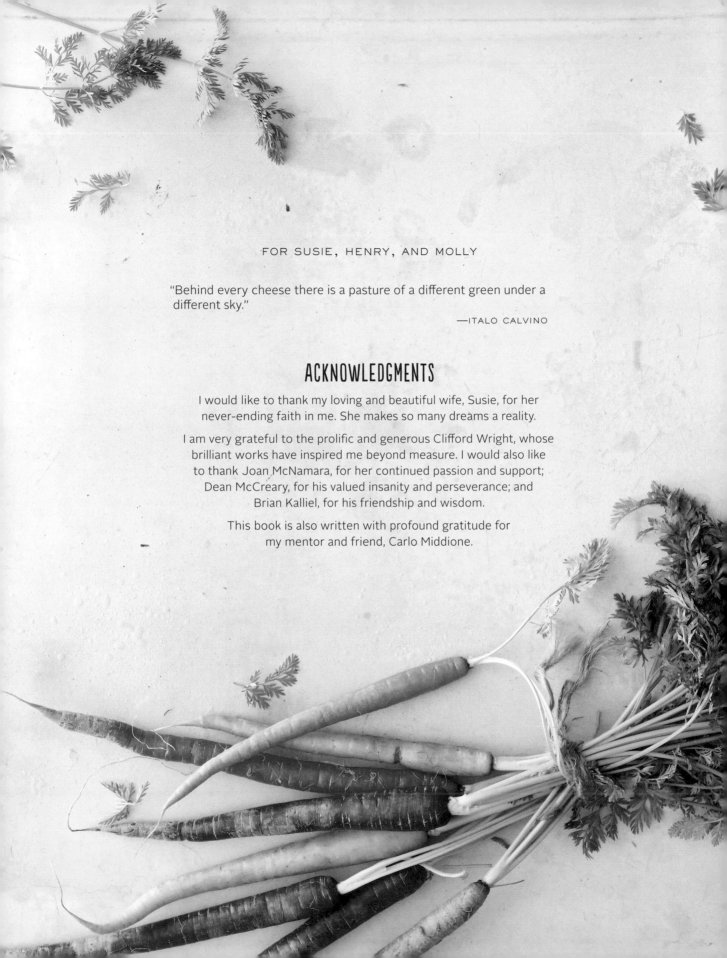

FOR SUSIE, HENRY, AND MOLLY

"Behind every cheese there is a pasture of a different green under a different sky."

—ITALO CALVINO

ACKNOWLEDGMENTS

I would like to thank my loving and beautiful wife, Susie, for her never-ending faith in me. She makes so many dreams a reality.

I am very grateful to the prolific and generous Clifford Wright, whose brilliant works have inspired me beyond measure. I would also like to thank Joan McNamara, for her continued passion and support; Dean McCreary, for his valued insanity and perseverance; and Brian Kalliel, for his friendship and wisdom.

This book is also written with profound gratitude for my mentor and friend, Carlo Middione.

FOREWORD

BY CLIFFORD A. WRIGHT

When I first met Chester Hastings twenty years ago, he was an apprentice to Master Chef Carlo Middione, who gave a dinner celebrating my first cookbook. Little did I realize that this young man not only would come to write cookbooks but that he would do so with a panache and suaveness that would open up a world of foods and seduce his readers into the kitchen. There is no greater joy than to have one's eyes opened to a subject that one believes one knows well. This is the effect *The Cheesemonger's Seasons* has had on me.

Cheese has come a long way in this country from the days—days that I remember in the late 1960s—when rubbery mozzarella, canned Parmesan, and cheese by-products such as Velveeta were the only offerings. Back then, there were no cheese stores, no artisanal cheese—or artisanal anything for that matter. Today, a wide world of cheese has arrived in our kitchens. Not only do we need a guide to introduce us to unfamiliar cheeses, we need *The Cheesemonger's Seasons* to teach us to cook with the array of cheeses that we can now readily find.

In his own *summa lacticiniorum,* Chester has continued a great tradition that began with the first treatise ever written on cheese, the *Summa lacticiniorum* by Pantaleone da Confienza, a professor at the University of Turin who published his veritable encyclopedia in 1459. Pantaleone's book is devoted to environmental, hygienic, dietetic, economic, and gastronomic aspects concerning the production of milk, and, above all, cheeses, whose extensive varieties are listed for the first time.

Echoing *La Formaggiata* published in 1542 by Guido Landi in honor of *cacio piacentino,* better known as Parmesan cheese, Chester says it all begins with grass. How else to understand the seasons of cheese, this marvelous food resulting from the magical transformation of milk? After grass comes milk, and after milk comes cheese; and in this book, those fabulous cheeses—now far more readily available than yester-year—are utilized in some of the most intriguing and enticing of recipes. Take for instance Coffee-Rubbed Leg of Lamb Stuffed with Spinach and Aged Cheddar, a dish about which Chester says, "I had been meaning to try cooking lamb with coffee for years." I read this recipe and nearly dropped everything to give it a try. And this was only one recipe. Every recipe in this book is like a persuasive carnival barker drawing you in unrelentingly.

When Chester writes about summer's arrival in the French Alps, when animals are moved to graze on higher pastures, where grasses they feed on are peppered with wildflowers that impart flavors to rich milk, you can almost taste it. Then you see, as you peruse this book, recipes that leap out and you can almost taste them they are so inviting. I write this in the spring, so I'm drawn to that section, as the book is divided by seasons, and I read about Little Gem Lettuces with Rogue River Blue, Agen Prunes, and Walnut Oil Vinaigrette; Spaetzle with Fried Onions and Beaufort d'Alpage; and Frittata with Dandelion Greens and Ossau Iraty. I am open-eyed and open-mouthed as I know I'm in the competent hands of a master cheesemonger and master cook.

Writing this foreword was difficult for me because this was one of those rare cookbooks that drew me away from my computer and pushed me toward my kitchen, such was the allure of these recipes. There is no better guide into the world of cheeses than Chester Hastings and *The Cheesemonger's Seasons*.

INTRODUCTION

In my first cookbook, *The Cheesemonger's Kitchen,* I stated that of all the chapters for cooking with cheese, "Vegetables" was the hardest chapter to whittle down. The possibilities for marrying top-quality produce with the world's finest cheeses are endless. The best recipes are often the simplest, as truly great cheese and ripe, in-season fruits and vegetables all share the character of being best appreciated as purely as can be. More important, cheese, like fresh fruits and many vegetables, should be cooked as little as possible. This kind of cooking epitomizes the key to re-creating the great cuisines of Western Europe: take very good ingredients and do very little to them.

The proliferation of farmers' markets and the availability of high-quality organic, seasonal, and local foods in grocery stores across the map are slowly improving the landscape of American and British diets. More and more top restaurants and local eateries are focusing on a Mediterranean approach to cooking: creatively using the best produce from reliable sources, always seeking to highlight the complex and glorious flavors of the garden.

The Dairy and the Garden

The heart of cheesemaking has always been the farm. Cheese is as much an agricultural product as it is an artisanal one. The humble and wholesome cooking of rural France, Italy, and Spain, as well as the farmstead kitchens of the United Kingdom and the United States, are replete with the traditional union of the pasture and the field.

Cheese begins first and foremost as grass, so it is only natural to pair it with spring's pods and stalks, summer's riot of fruits, autumn's treasures of the vine, and winter's nutrient-rich leaves and roots. I often turn to the farming communities where the cheeses I love are produced to see what the people of the land themselves do with their own creations. It is the kind of culinary anthropology that was instilled in me by my mentor, Carlo Middione. The traditional cooking methods and recipes of cheesemaking cultures can go a long way in informing us all on how to cook with cheeses from around the world. And while a specific cheese or type of produce called for in a recipe may not always be available to us, by looking at the flavor combinations within a classic dish, we can find inspiration for choosing similar style cheeses or vegetables from other areas with a like mind toward creating and combining flavors.

The serving of fruit and cheese is classic the world over, especially at breakfast. The combination is a rich source of protein and vitamins, but, beyond this, the serenity, simplicity, and pleasure of a morning with great cheese and ripe fruit can set the tone for the whole day. Of course, fruit is not reserved for just breakfast or dessert, and far beyond the direct experience of the cheeses on the board, there is something akin to alchemy about sticky ripe figs stuffed with tangy goat cheese, clothed in an elegant robe of gamey bresaola, or bright wild strawberries tossed into a creamy risotto finished with a dollop of soft cow's-milk robiola. These dishes exemplify pure and perfect elements brought together in a balance of flavor, texture, and passion.

Seasonal Cooking

Cooking by the seasons is made easier with a map of the world. In the colder winter months, I am often drawn to the cuisines of the Alpine regions of Italy, France, and Switzerland, as well as the hearth-bound foods of Great Britain. Springtime brings me to the vibrant cooking of central Italy and southwest France, and the scorching hot days of summer can be mediated by the light and sometimes spicy cooking of southern Italy and much of Spain. Thus, a repertoire of techniques and recipes emerges filled with simple, traditional dishes that are hearty when they need to be and refreshing when the weather calls for it.

In the modern food-gathering experience, we are so used to finding strawberries in January, even if they don't have any taste, that it is often hard to define the seasons with the foods that best suit them. Enter the local farmers' market. A weekly stroll through the caravans of honest, humble food growers hocking their treasures with a spirit of unabashed community rarely seen elsewhere can reap rewards far greater than a bounty of ripe fruit and healthful veggies. An hour or two spent wandering the market with friends and family, seeing the faces and talking to the very people whose love and passion have gone into the foods we are about to eat, is a vital human experience we must try to continue. It is here, with the naked eye and heightened senses, that we can see, taste, and smell what the season truly is on any given day. It is a ritual that many of the world's top chefs insist upon before designing their ever-changing menus. Using the farmers' market as a kind of almanac in this way is a far more inspiring and practical approach to cooking than all the cookbook reading and magazine flipping in the world. And the same holds true for cheese, as a regular visit to, and dialogue with, your local cheese-monger will keep you well informed about what is in season and at its peak.

Seasons of Cheese

While there is a wide world of cheeses that are read-ily available year-round, in particular the longer-aged cheeses such Parmigiano-Reggiano, Grana-style grating cheeses, Gruyères, Cheddars, Goudas, and many pecorinos, there are quite a few fresh cheeses that are made during a small window of time, and the window for enjoying them is just as small.

Amazingly, you will often find that many of these specialty cheeses are perfectly ripe about the same time that the fruits and vegetables they pair best with are showing up in the markets. For example, fresh goat and sheep's-milk cheeses come about in early spring, when pasture grasses studded with wildflowers and herbs are more abundant and sweet. The milk from animals grazing on this diet is much richer, with a higher fat content than the hay-fed animals in other seasons or in the larger factory dairies. Delicate fresh cheeses are at their peak during this time, although they often remain delicious throughout the summer. Many of those pecorinos made in winter are just now coming out of the caves. At about the same time, we find fresh fava beans and English peas, young asparagus, and tender salad greens popping up in the marketplace or backyard garden beds—foods that are particularly suited to balancing these cheeses marvelously. Nature herself is already in the business of food pairing!

Conversely, while there is little grazing to be had in the winter, and therefore traditionally less-flavorful milk produced during this time, those cold days are when many of the cheeses that were made in the summer are just coming into their own. The few months of aging have developed some of the more subtle flavors found in summer milk, often influenced heavily by the natural or manipulated environment the cheese is aged in. The colder weather also calls for richer comfort food, and it is these cheeses, like Epoisses, Camembert, and virtually all of the blues, that are not only ripe and ready, but are perfect for the celebratory season of hearty holiday cooking.

The following recipes comprise a collection of some of my favorite ways to explore great cheeses with the seasonal fruits and vegetables that comple-ment them so well. They are organized into chapters by season, then are grouped by produce type. They come from my own experiences both traveling the world and exploring my own imagination. I encourage you to do both as often as you can to discover a closer connection with the food you eat and serve to those you love.

A Note about Temperatures for Cheese
When serving fine cheeses on their own, it is always best to first bring them to room temperature, so the cheese is at its optimum texture and the fullest flavors are brought out. In preparing these recipes, unless otherwise stated, keep the cheese cold until you're ready to use it. For grating cheeses such as Parmigiano-Reggiano, however, it is a good idea to bring them to room temperature as well before grating and adding to the dish.

SPRING

Breakfast Radishes with Triple-Cream Cheese 16

**Nasturtium Leaves with French Feta, Pine Nuts,
and Smoked Paprika** 18

**Little Gem Lettuces with Rogue River Blue, Agen Prunes,
and Walnut Oil Vinaigrette** 21

**Pea Shoots with Burrata, Lemon Olive Oil,
and Toasted Sesame Seeds** 22

Raw Baby Artichoke Salad with Pecorino Toscano 24

Focaccia with Slivered Artichokes and Goat Cheese 26

Arugula Salad with Sovrano Cheese and Pears 28

Panini with Arugula and Honey Bee Goat Gouda 29

**Crostini with Fava Bean Purée, Fresh Pecorino,
Crispy Shallot, and Pistachios** 30

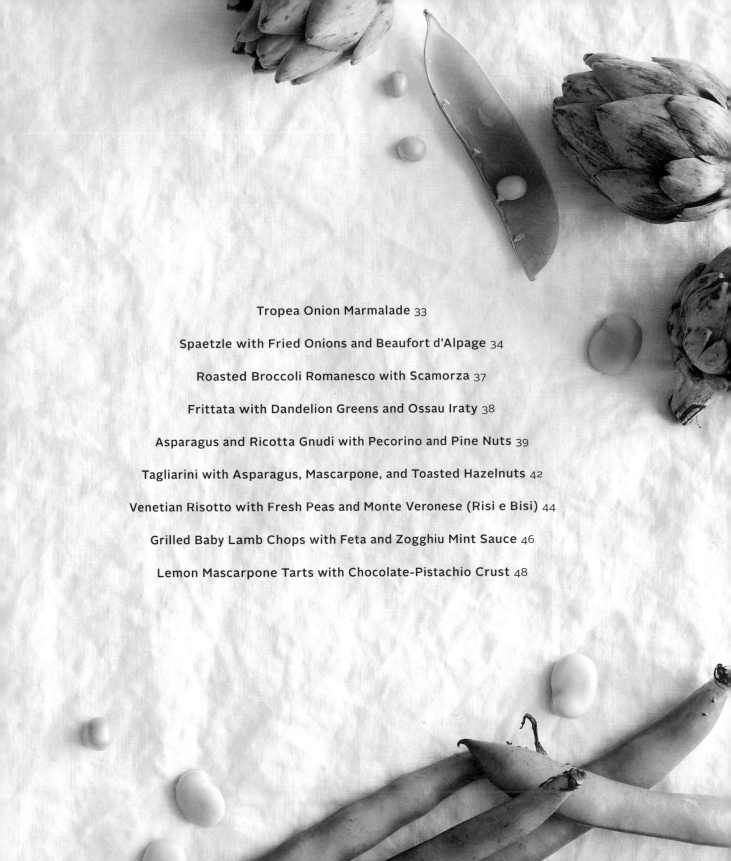

Tropea Onion Marmalade 33

Spaetzle with Fried Onions and Beaufort d'Alpage 34

Roasted Broccoli Romanesco with Scamorza 37

Frittata with Dandelion Greens and Ossau Iraty 38

Asparagus and Ricotta Gnudi with Pecorino and Pine Nuts 39

Tagliarini with Asparagus, Mascarpone, and Toasted Hazelnuts 42

Venetian Risotto with Fresh Peas and Monte Veronese (Risi e Bisi) 44

Grilled Baby Lamb Chops with Feta and Zogghiu Mint Sauce 46

Lemon Mascarpone Tarts with Chocolate-Pistachio Crust 48

BREAKFAST RADISHES WITH TRIPLE-CREAM CHEESE

SERVES 4 TO 6

7 oz/200 g Délice de Crémiers, Brillat-Savarin, or other soft-ripened triple-cream cheese

14 fresh French breakfast or rainbow radishes, scrubbed

While in France earlier this year, my family and I were hard pressed not to buy every morsel of raw, ripe cheese we knew we would never see Stateside (at least not until Americans get realistic about some of the restrictive food laws we subscribe to).

Our self-control does have its limits, however. We were faced with an abundance of really ripe, extra-silky Délice de Crémiers, the soft-ripened triple-cream cow's-milk cheese that is also 75 percent butterfat! The French tradition of eating crisp, peppery breakfast radishes with farm butter and sea salt inspired us to try our radishes with the already salty and highly buttery cheese . . . and it was heaven, pure and simple. Brillat-Savarin triple-cream cheese is also a perfect substitute.

This is a great addition to a cheese board. Surround the wheel of cheese with a rainbow pile of pastel radishes, or make delightful tea sandwiches on a nutty grain bread or simple *pain de mie*.

Bring the cheese to room temperature on a decorative plate or cheese board. (Délice de Crémiers is sold in lovely round balsa wood boxes, which I find is the perfect serving dish.) Arrange the radishes in a pretty display alongside the cheese, leaving any nice-looking leaves attached. Serve immediately.

NASTURTIUM LEAVES WITH FRENCH FETA, PINE NUTS, AND SMOKED PAPRIKA

SERVES 4 TO 6

2 oz/55 g feta cheese, preferably French

1 tbsp pine nuts, toasted

12 large nasturtium leaves

Smoked paprika for sprinkling

1 tbsp extra-virgin olive oil

Nasturtium flowers for garnish (optional)

Nasturtiums have taken over my front yard—and I love it. They are such a friendly flower, and a handful of them in an old glass jam jar is more lovely to me than a dozen roses. They are edible, and as such brighten up salads on our table in a powerful way as well. But what's perhaps less known is it's not just the flowers that have value in the kitchen: the lily pad–like leaves of the nasturtium plant pack a delightful peppery kick, and can be used to liven up salad greens, create a spicy pesto, or, as in this case, wrap around creamy cheese for a special appetizer.

These free-form bites are visually stunning and pair nicely with a rosé or crisp white wine before dinner. The recipe multiplies easily for larger parties. A good, strong pinch of the leaves around the cheese is usually enough to keep them stuck closed.

Keep a tin of good-quality Spanish smoked paprika in your cupboard. A little goes a very long way, and this evocative spice with its smoky flavor and gentle kick is invaluable on many vegetables and meats.

In a small bowl, combine the feta and pine nuts and stir to mix, breaking up the cheese into small bits with a fork. Set aside.

Wash and dry the nasturtium leaves carefully. Lay them, darker-side down, on a clean work surface and spoon the feta mixture into the center of each leaf, dividing it evenly.

Sprinkle a very small amount of the smoked paprika, literally a dash per leaf, onto the feta. Dot small drops of the olive oil on the paprika.

Firmly gather the edges of the leaves together with your fingertips and squeeze to enclose the cheese, creating a kind of rough four-cornered hat shape. If any part of the leaf won't stay up, just pinch a little harder. They should all look a little rough and not perfect, which adds to their natural beauty. (The nasturtium bundles can be assembled up to 1 hour in advance and refrigerated. Bring to room temperature before serving.)

To serve, arrange the bundles on a serving plate, garnished with some nasturtium flowers, if you like.

Little Gem is a baby romaine-type lettuce with a unique delicate quality—more like a cross between romaine and butter (Boston) lettuce. In France, they are known as Sucrine, for their sweet flavor. The versatile little guys are also ideal for braising or grilling, like radicchio. They make a stunning appearance in salads when the heads are separated but the leaves left whole.

Prunes and walnuts have had a fantastic love affair for centuries, especially in southwest France. The famous prunes from Agen have a deep black color and an Old World flavor that cannot be replicated, incredible with aged and blue cheeses. But plum farmers all over are offering heirloom varieties at their local markets, and any of these will be phenomenal with blue cheeses like the one featured here, Oregon's pride and joy, Rogue River Blue.

TO MAKE THE VINAIGRETTE: In a small jar with a tight-fitting lid, combine the walnut oil, vinegar, honey, and mustard and season with salt and pepper. Close the jar and shake vigorously until thoroughly blended and a thick, smooth dressing forms. Taste and adjust the seasoning. Set aside.

Separate all of the lettuce leaves. Rinse and dry well. Snap off any tough stems. Place the whole lettuce leaves in a large serving bowl. Crumble in the cheese and add the prunes. Drizzle in just enough of the vinaigrette to lightly coat the leaves and toss gently.

Serve immediately, right from the serving bowl. Or, to plate individually, omit the cheese and prunes from the dressing step, and gently stack the dressed leaves on individual plates, then scatter the prunes and crumbled cheese over them.

LITTLE GEM LETTUCES WITH ROGUE RIVER BLUE, AGEN PRUNES, AND WALNUT OIL VINAIGRETTE

SERVES 4

FOR THE VINAIGRETTE:

¼ cup/60 ml walnut oil

2 tbsp red wine vinegar

2 tbsp mild, creamy honey such as lavender or white honey

1 tsp Dijon mustard

Sea salt and freshly cracked black pepper

2 to 4 Little Gem lettuces, or a mixture of hearts of romaine and butter (Boston) lettuce

2 oz/55 g Rogue River Blue or other soft creamy blue cheese

4 or 5 pitted Agen prunes, sliced

When I was visiting Princess Marina Colonna many years ago in Rome, she was in the process of developing a line of citrus-infused olive oils, and tasked my mentor, Carlo, and me with developing a few recipes featuring these exotic creations.

"Infused" is not really the right word here, however, as these oils are made by crushing whole citrus fruits (peels, seeds, and all) with the olives at the time of pressing to create a blend of oil so deeply permeated with fruit it will blow your mind. Agrumato, in Abruzzo, is another producer who uses the same technique to create a variety of oils that are outstanding for drizzling raw over grilled vegetables, fish, chicken, and salad greens.

If you can't get your hands on a lemon olive oil for this recipe, use a good fruity extra-virgin olive oil and add freshly squeezed lemon juice to taste. There should be a nice balance of acidity to fat.

Toast the sesame seeds in a small, dry skillet over medium heat for about 1 minute, until just barely turning golden, taking care not to burn them. Remove from the heat and immediately pour the seeds into a small bowl. Let cool completely.

Trim any tough lower leaves from the pea shoots, then rinse and dry well.

Cut the Burrata into four equal pieces and lay them, cut-sides up, on a serving platter or four individual plates.

Divide the pea shoots evenly around the Burrata pieces. Drizzle the olive oil over the pea shoots and Burrata and scatter the sesame seeds over the top. Season with salt and pepper. Serve immediately.

PEA SHOOTS WITH BURRATA, LEMON OLIVE OIL, AND TOASTED SESAME SEEDS

SERVES 4

2 tbsp sesame seeds

2 cups/115 g fresh pea shoots

1 lb/455 g fresh Burrata cheese

4 tbsp/60 ml lemon-infused olive oil

Sea salt and freshly cracked black pepper

RAW BABY ARTICHOKE SALAD WITH PECORINO TOSCANO

SERVES 6 TO 8

FOR THE VINAIGRETTE:

½ cup/120 ml extra-virgin olive oil

½ cup/120 ml fresh lemon juice

1 small shallot, thinly sliced

3 anchovy fillets

Sea salt and freshly cracked black pepper

2 lb/910 g baby artichokes

¼ cup/7 g fresh flat-leaf (Italian) parsley leaves

2 tbsp capers, drained and roughly chopped

6 oz/170 g Pecorino Toscano Stagionato or other aged hard sheep's-milk cheese, cut into shavings with a vegetable peeler or the large slot of a box grater

This is one of those incredible antipasti one finds lined up on the sideboard of a simple trattoria in Italy. Raw young artichokes have a unique flavor and fantastic texture, and they marry wonderfully with the great aged Pecorinos of Tuscany.

When selecting baby artichokes, take the time to find small, firm, tightly closed ones, which are the best for eating raw.

TO MAKE THE VINAIGRETTE: In a small jar with a tight-fitting lid, combine the olive oil, lemon juice, shallot, and anchovy fillets. Close the jar tightly and shake vigorously until thoroughly blended and a thick, smooth dressing forms. Season with salt and pepper and set aside.

To clean the artichokes, snap off the tough outer leaves until you get to the pale yellow inner leaves. Using a sharp knife, peel the skin from the stems and cut the artichokes in half lengthwise. Turn the halves cut-side down, and cut lengthwise into very thin slices. Immediately transfer to a large bowl, add the parsley leaves and capers, and toss to mix. Drizzle in the dressing and toss to coat.

Transfer the salad to a serving plate, then scatter the Pecorino shavings over the top. Serve at room temperature.

FOCACCIA WITH SLIVERED ARTICHOKES AND GOAT CHEESE

MAKES ONE 12-BY-16-IN/30.5-BY-40.5-CM FOCACCIA

FOR THE DOUGH:

1½ cups/360 ml lukewarm water

2¼ tsp active dry yeast

½ tsp sea salt

½ tsp sugar

3½ cups/450 g all-purpose flour

2 tbsp extra-virgin olive oil

1 lemon, halved

1 lb/455 g baby artichokes

10 tbsp/150 ml extra-virgin olive oil

Spring vegetables, including and especially young baby artichokes quickly cooked until just tender, are a perfect topping for pizzas and focaccia, and are beautiful to boot.

I am very fond of mixing fresh oregano and mint with artichokes to emulate the flavor of the Roman wild mint known as *mentuccia,* which is used to make the famous *carciofi alla Romana.* It is an herbal combination that happens to be sublime with fresh goat cheese.

TO MAKE THE DOUGH: Pour the warm water into a large bowl. Sprinkle the yeast on the surface of the water, along with the salt and sugar. Let stand for 5 minutes, or until the yeast is dissolved and creamy, then add 1¾ cups/225 g of the flour. Stir with a wooden spoon until all the flour is incorporated and a very wet and sticky starter dough forms. Place a kitchen towel over the bowl and let stand at room temperature until it has increased in bulk by about one-third, about 2 hours.

Uncover the bowl and add the remaining 1¾ cups/225 g flour, along with 1 tbsp of the olive oil. Using a wooden spoon, stir until most of the flour is incorporated, then turn the dough out onto a generously floured work surface. Knead the dough, dusting your hands and the board with more flour as needed to prevent sticking, until the dough is still slightly sticky but elastic, with a nice spring when you touch it, 5 to 10 minutes. Pat the dough into a ball, return it to the bowl, and rub all over with the remaining 1 tbsp olive oil. Re-cover and rest until doubled in bulk, about 1 hour longer.

Meanwhile, squeeze the juice from 1 lemon half into a bowl of water and set aside. Clean the artichokes by snapping off the tough outer leaves until you get to the pale yellow inner leaves. Using a sharp knife, peel the skin from the stems and cut the artichokes in half lengthwise. Turn the halves cut-side down, and cut lengthwise into very thin slices. Immediately transfer the slivered artichokes to the bowl of lemon water.

Heat 4 tbsp/60 ml of the olive oil in a large sauté pan or skillet over medium heat. Add the onion and stir to coat with the oil. Drain the artichokes, pat dry on a kitchen towel, and add to the pan with the onion. Sauté for about 10 minutes, until the onion is slightly golden and the artichokes are tender. Squeeze the juice from the remaining lemon half over the artichokes and onion, remove from the heat, and let cool to room temperature. (The artichokes and onion can be prepared to this point up to 3 hours in advance.)

Turn the dough out onto a lightly floured work surface. Using the your fingertips and the palms of your hands, press and stretch out the dough to form a 12-by-16-in/30.5-by-40.5-cm rectangle. The dough will be quite springy, so let it rest a bit between stretching. Grease a baking sheet with 2 tbsp of the olive oil. Transfer the dough to the oiled pan and, using only your fingertips, push the dough back out as needed to reshape the 12-by-16-in/30.5-by-40.5-cm rectangle, then press all over, allowing your fingertips to form deep imprints. Scatter the crushed garlic over the top of the dough, then spread on the cooled onion and artichokes. Crumble the goat cheese over the top and sprinkle the oregano and mint all over. Cover lightly with a kitchen towel and let rest for 20 minutes. Preheat the oven to 400°F/200°C.

Uncover the focaccia and drizzle the remaining 4 tbsp/60 ml olive oil over the entire surface. Sprinkle with the Parmigiano and season with salt and pepper. Bake for 25 to 30 minutes, or until the bottom is golden brown and the top is lightly browned around the edges.

Let cool slightly, then cut into squares and serve warm or at room temperature.

1 small yellow onion, thinly sliced

6 garlic cloves, crushed

8 oz/225 g fresh goat cheese

1 tbsp chopped fresh oregano

1 tbsp chopped fresh mint

4 oz/115 g Parmigiano-Reggiano cheese, grated

Sea salt and freshly cracked black pepper

Sovrano is a grana-style cheese—that is, hard and crumbly, with a distinctive granular texture—from Lombardy in northern Italy, made from a mixture of water buffalo's milk and cow's milk. It is a slightly milder cheese than its grana cousins Grana Padano and Parmigiano-Reggiano, but has a full fruity flavor and a dramatic bone-white color that contrast beautifully on both counts with the bitter dark green arugula leaves.

Arugula and pear salads have in many ways become a standard the world over, but the use of Sovrano in lieu of the more typical Parmigiano-Reggiano, while a subtle difference, is one that I find works well to highlight the best of all the ingredients.

ARUGULA SALAD WITH SOVRANO CHEESE AND PEARS

SERVES 4 TO 6

FOR THE VINAIGRETTE:

¼ cup/60 ml extra-virgin olive oil

2 tbsp fresh lemon juice, or more if needed

1 tbsp thinly sliced fresh basil

Sea salt and freshly cracked black pepper

2 small, ripe juicy pears such as Comice or Anjou

8 oz/225 g baby arugula

3 oz/85 g Sovrano cheese, cut into shavings with a vegetable peeler or the large slot of a box grater

TO MAKE THE VINAIGRETTE: In a small jar with a tight-fitting lid, combine the olive oil, lemon juice, and basil. Close the jar tightly and shake vigorously until thoroughly blended and a thick, smooth dressing forms. Season with a good pinch of salt and pepper, and more lemon juice, if needed. Set aside.

Peel, halve, and core the pears. Cut each half into thin slices and place in a large bowl. Add the arugula and toss gently to mix, then add the dressing and toss to coat. Transfer the dressed arugula and pears to a large serving bowl or divide among individual plates. Scatter the cheese shavings over the salads and serve immediately.

Honey Bee Goat Gouda comes from a cheesemaker in the Netherlands. It is a goat's-milk cheese that is rubbed with honey to impart a touch of caramel-like sweetness to the finished cheese—a characteristic that contrasts nicely with peppery raw arugula. Other goat's-milk Goudas or Cheddars would also work nicely.

This is one of those simple sandwiches for which the quality of the few ingredients is paramount, so find a good, nutty, whole-grain rustic bread from your local bakery for starters. I love this toasted sandwich for an afternoon snack with a strong cup of tea.

Preheat a sandwich grill, or place a large sauté pan or skillet over medium heat.

Lay the bread out on a work surface and layer the cheese over two of the slices, dividing it evenly. Distribute the arugula evenly over the cheese, then top with the remaining two bread slices.

Drizzle 1 tsp of the olive oil on each top bread slice, and carefully transfer the assembled panini, oil-side down, to the hot grill or pan. Drizzle 1 tsp of the remaining olive oil over each bottom bread slice and close the lid on the press, or press down on the panini with a metal spatula, if using a pan.

Cook until the bread is toasted to a nice golden brown and the cheese is thoroughly melted, 5 to 7 minutes. If using the pan, flip over the panini half-way through the cooking time. Cut in half and serve immediately.

PANINI WITH ARUGULA AND HONEY BEE GOAT GOUDA

SERVES 2

4 slices rustic whole-grain bread

4 oz/115 g Honey Bee or other goat's-milk Gouda cheese, shredded

2 handfuls of baby arugula

4 tsp extra-virgin olive oil

CROSTINI WITH FAVA BEAN PURÉE, FRESH PECORINO, CRISPY SHALLOT, AND PISTACHIOS

SERVES 12 TO 15

1 lb/455 g fresh fava beans, shelled

12 tbsp/180 ml extra-virgin olive oil

1 garlic clove

Sea salt and freshly cracked black pepper

½ cup/120 ml water

Zest of 1 lemon

1 large shallot, thinly sliced

½ baguette, cut into ¼-in-/6-mm-thick slices

9 oz/255 g fresh pecorino or other semisoft sheep's-milk cheese, thinly sliced

1 oz/30 g raw pistachios, finely chopped

In Italy, young fava beans are often eaten raw, accompanied with a sharp and salty pecorino, but they are even more elegant cooked *in umido,* as the Italians say, a kind of quick braising in liquid made of fruity olive oil, a little garlic, and just enough water to keep them moist.

Throughout late spring and all the way through the hot summer months, soft-skinned, tender-fleshed fava bean pods can be found piled high on our kitchen table. These crostini are a perfect appetizer to awaken the taste buds; serve at a cocktail party or with a crisp glass of white wine or Prosecco before a dinner of grilled fish or chicken.

Bring a medium saucepan of water to a boil over high heat. Add the fava beans to the boiling water and cook for 1 minute to loosen the thin inner skins. Drain the beans in a colander and let stand just until cool enough to handle. Peel the warm beans by tearing the skins and squeezing the beans out into a small bowl.

Heat 2 tbsp of the olive oil and the garlic clove together in a sauté pan or skillet over medium-high heat. Cook the garlic until lightly golden on both sides, taking care not to allow the oil to smoke. Add the skinned fava beans and sauté 1 to 2 minutes. Season with salt and pepper. Add the water, reduce the heat to low, and simmer for about 5 minutes longer, or until most of the liquid is gone and the beans are very tender. (If the beans are still too firm by the time the water is gone, add a splash more water and cook until it is absorbed.)

Discard the garlic clove. Transfer the fava beans to a food processor fitted with the blade attachment and process to a smooth purée. Transfer to a bowl. Add the lemon zest and 3 tbsp of the olive oil and stir to mix well. Taste and adjust the seasoning. (The purée can be made up to 2 hours ahead of time and kept at room temperature until needed, or up to 1 day in advance—cover and refrigerate, then bring to room temperature before serving.)

cont'd

Heat 2 tbsp of the olive oil in a small sauté pan or skillet over medium heat until hot but not smoking. Add the shallot and cook, stirring often with a fork or tongs to break up the rings and prevent burning, for about 3 minutes or until nicely browned and crunchy. Remove from the heat and transfer the shallot rings to paper towels to drain.

Meanwhile, preheat the oven to 450°F/230°C. Place the baguette slices on a baking sheet and drizzle evenly with the remaining 5 tbsp/75 ml olive oil. Bake for about 7 minutes, or until golden and crisp. Remove from the oven and let cool.

Distribute the pecorino evenly over the cooled toasts. Spoon about 1 tsp of the fava bean purée atop each slice of cheese, followed by a few rings of crispy shallot. Top with a sprinkling of the chopped pistachios and serve immediately.

Tropea onions are long, red, sweet onions that originated in Calabria, in southern Italy. They have a deep flavor that is well suited for grilling or caramelizing, and it is this complex onion essence that stands out against the sweetness of a marmalade. Torpedo or other red onion varieties will work as well, but if you come across a pile of the Tropea at your local farmers' market, buy a bunch and see what all the fuss is about.

Use this marmalade for all intents and purposes as you would chutney. It is great with aged cheeses like Parmigiano-Reggiano, Gouda, and Cheddar, as well as soft Taleggio or creamy goat cheese.

Soak the raisins in warm water to cover for 10 minutes until rehydrated. Drain and squeeze tightly to remove any excess water. Roughly chop the raisins and set aside.

Heat the olive oil in a large sauté pan or skillet over medium-high heat until hot but not smoking. Add the onions and season with salt and pepper. Sauté for about 5 minutes, or until the onions are beginning to soften and turn golden around the edges. Add the sugar and stir well to coat the onions. Raise the heat to high and add the wine. Bring the mixture to a boil, then reduce the heat to maintain a gentle simmer. Cook until the onions are caramelized to a rich brown color and the mixture has taken on a thick, jamlike consistency, 12 to 15 minutes.

Remove from the heat and let cool slightly, then transfer to a clean glass jar or other container with an airtight lid. Let cool completely before covering tightly. Refrigerate until ready to serve. The marmalade will keep, tightly covered in the refrigerator, for up to 2 weeks.

TROPEA ONION MARMALADE

MAKES 1½ CUPS/340 G

3 tbsp golden raisins

3 tbsp extra-virgin olive oil

2 lb/910 g Tropea or other small red onions, thinly sliced

Sea salt and freshly cracked black pepper

1½ cups/300 g sugar

¾ cup/180 ml dry white wine

SPAETZLE WITH FRIED ONIONS AND BEAUFORT D'ALPAGE

SERVES 4 TO 6

FOR THE SPAETZLE:

3 cups/385 g all-purpose flour

Sea salt and freshly cracked black pepper

4 large eggs

1½ cups/360 ml whole milk

8 tbsp/115 g unsalted butter

2 medium yellow onions, thinly sliced

8 oz/225 g Beaufort d'Alpage or Gruyère de Comté cheese

When summer arrives in the French Alps, the herds and flocks of mountain animals are moved to graze on higher pastures, where the grasses are peppered with high-altitude wildflowers. It is believed that this movement creates a richer, creamier milk, not to mention the incredible flavors imparted from the special diet.

While most mountain cheeses are made down in the lower valleys, there are some that are actually made and aged in small chalets high up in the mountains where the shepherds, cheesemakers, and even the animals sleep at night. These cheeses are called "Alpage."

Beaufort d' Alpage is one such cheese, and while there are outstanding Beauforts to be had year-round, the Alpage variety, aged 6 months or more, is certainly worth trying when you see it in late winter and early spring. The wild-flower and grassy flavors are immediately apparent, and deepen the complexity of this otherwise very simple classic German dish.

TO MAKE THE SPAETZLE: In a large bowl, whisk together the flour, 2 tsp salt, and a few grindings of pepper. Make a well in the center. Break the eggs into the center of the well and add the milk. Using a fork, beat the eggs and milk together. Continue beating, and begin to pull flour from the sides of the well a little at a time. Gradually add more flour from the well to the mix as you work, until all of the flour is incorporated. (You may need to add a touch more flour or milk; you want a sticky batter that is still loose enough to push through the holes of a spaetzle maker.)

Bring a large pot of water to a boil over high heat and add a small handful of salt. Have ready a small bowl of water and ice.

When the water is boiling, put about ½ cup/ 115 g of the batter in the spaetzle maker or a colander. Using a rubber spatula, push the batter through the holes directly into the boiling water and cook until the spaetzle float and look plump and firm, 1 to 2 minutes. Using a strainer or slotted spoon, plunge the spaetzle into the ice water to stop the cooking, then immediately drain and transfer to a large bowl. Repeat to cook the remaining batter.

cont'd

(The spaetzle can be made to this point up to 3 hours ahead. Toss with a little melted butter or a drizzle of extra-virgin olive oil to prevent them from sticking and set aside at room temperature.)

Next, melt 2 tbsp of the butter in a large sauté pan or skillet over medium-low heat. Add the onions and cook, stirring occasionally, until they are deep golden brown and crispy, 12 to 15 minutes. Remove from the heat and set aside.

When ready to serve, melt the remaining 6 tbsp/85 g butter in another large sauté pan over high heat. Add the spaetzle and sauté, shaking the pan from time to time, allowing little golden spots to appear here and there. Remove from the heat, crumble the cheese over the spaetzle, and stir to combine well. Transfer to a warmed serving dish, top with the crispy onions, and serve immediately.

More tender than either cauliflower or broccoli (with a delightful resemblance to both) vibrant green broccoli Romanesco, or "Roman cauliflower," needs very little cooking. It is one of my favorite vegetables to enjoy raw, but when cooking it, as with zucchini, high heat for a short time delivers the right tender bite and golden edges. In this recipe, the salty flavors and smoky aromas of Scamorza cheese are a perfect match.

Scamorza is a cow's-milk cheese that belongs to the same family as mozzarella and provolone, with equally good melting properties. It is made plain or gently smoked, and is tied with ropes before hanging to form a pear shape. In Sicily, this cheese is called *caciocavallo* for its resemblance to saddlebags; in other parts of southern Italy, it is said that the name invokes the word *scamozza,* used to describe someone who has been beheaded—the baglike appearance of the cheese apparently resembled a head in a sack for those who had seen their fair share.

Position a rack in the upper third of the oven and preheat to 450°F/230°C.

Using the tip of a small knife, break the Romanesco into small florets. Cut the core and stems into pieces about the same size as the florets. Put all the Romanesco in a large bowl and drizzle with the olive oil. Add the parsley, cheese, and bread crumbs and toss gently to mix. Season with salt and pepper.

Transfer the Romanesco to a rimmed baking sheet. Roast in the upper part of the oven, stirring once halfway through, until golden on the edges and tender, about 20 minutes. Serve immediately.

ROASTED BROCCOLI ROMANESCO WITH SCAMORZA

SERVES 4

1 head broccoli Romanesco

3 tbsp extra-virgin olive oil

¼ cup/10 g roughly chopped fresh flat-leaf (Italian) parsley

4 oz/115 g smoked Scamorza or smoked provolone cheese, shredded

¼ cup/30 g dried bread crumbs

Sea salt and freshly cracked black pepper

FRITTATA WITH DANDELION GREENS AND OSSAU IRATY

SERVES 2

4 oz/115 g dandelion greens

2 tbsp extra-virgin olive oil

1 garlic clove, chopped

Sea salt and freshly cracked black pepper

6 large eggs

3 oz/85 g Ossau Iraty or other semihard sheep's-milk cheese, shredded

Dandelion greens quickly sautéed in extra-virgin olive oil with a touch of garlic are amazing simply as a side dish to fish, chicken, or pork. But here they are the stars of a savory frittata. The sweet, nutty flavors of a semihard sheep's milk cheese like Ossau Iraty from the French Pyrenees are a perfect balance to the delightful bitter bite of the greens. Enjoy this frittata as a light dinner for two, or cut into smaller wedges and serve as an antipasto with some olives and salami.

Preheat the oven to 500°F/260°C.

Wash the dandelion greens and dry thoroughly with a clean kitchen towel. Heat a medium ovenproof sauté pan or skillet over medium-high heat. Add the olive oil and swirl to coat the pan bottom. Add the greens and garlic, season well with salt and pepper, and sauté for 2 or 3 minutes, or until the garlic is just turning golden and the greens are wilted.

In a bowl, lightly beat the eggs. Add the cheese and beat vigorously with a fork before pouring into the hot pan. Stir quickly to distribute the greens among the eggs, then transfer the pan to the oven. Bake until the frittata is firm and puffed up nicely, 7 to 10 minutes.

Remove from the oven and shake the pan to loosen the frittata. Slide out onto a dinner plate, cut into wedges, and serve hot or at room temperature.

This is a Tuscan take on the humble gnocchi. Literally translated as "naked," *gnudi* are tender dumplings—basically ravioli filling without the pasta. Most often made with fresh ricotta and sautéed spinach, *gnudi* can be quite versatile, depending on the season. Beet greens, Swiss chard, even nettles can be simply cooked, squeezed of excess water, and added to the best ricotta you can get your hands on. *Gnudi* fall under the category of *malfatti,* or "poorly made" pastas in Italy, which means that they needn't be perfect spheres, and, like the best foods in life, should actually look and feel handmade.

The Callahan family of Bellwether Farms in Sonoma, California, produces a truly magnificent ricotta that works wonders with this recipe. You can find it or other fine small-batch ricottas in many quality grocers and cheese shops.

Bring a large pot of water to a boil over high heat and add a small handful of salt. Add the asparagus and cook until tender but still slightly firm to the bite, 3 to 4 minutes. Remove the pot from the heat. Using a slotted spoon or wire skimmer, transfer the asparagus to a colander; reserve the water to cook the gnudi in later. Immediately place the asparagus under cold running water to stop the cooking, then drain and pat dry on a kitchen towel.

Finely chop the asparagus and transfer to a bowl. Add the ricotta, bread crumbs, and Pecorino, and season with salt and pepper. Gently mix together until well combined.

Dust a baking sheet liberally with flour. Flour your hands well, too, then form the gnudi by taking up walnut-size pieces of the ricotta mixture in your fingers and rolling them into balls between your palms. Roll the shaped dumplings in the flour on the baking sheet to coat lightly and arrange them on the baking sheet so they don't touch.

Return the pot of water to high heat and bring back to a boil. Working in batches to avoid crowding the pot, add the gnudi and stir gently to prevent sticking. Let the water return to a boil, then reduce

cont'd

ASPARAGUS AND RICOTTA GNUDI WITH PECORINO AND PINE NUTS

MAKES 80 TO 90 *GNUDI*; SERVES 4 TO 6

Sea salt

14 oz/400 g young asparagus, tough woody ends removed, cut into pieces about 2 in/5 cm long

1 lb/455 g good-quality fresh ricotta

1¼ cups/140 g dried bread crumbs

3½ oz/100 g Pecorino Romano cheese, grated, plus more for serving

Freshly cracked black pepper

All-purpose flour for dusting

the heat to achieve a gentle simmer. Cook the gnudi for 2 to 3 minutes, or until they float to the surface. Transfer to a colander placed in the sink to drain as they are finished. Bring the water back to a boil between batches.

Meanwhile, in a large sauté pan or skillet over medium heat, combine the butter, pine nuts, and sage. Cook, stirring often, until the butter is melted and starting to brown and the pine nuts are nicely toasted, about 2 minutes.

When all of the gnudi are cooked, add them to the pan with the butter sauce. Raise the heat to medium-high and cook for a minute or so, until the dumplings have some golden edges. Serve immediately. Pass more grated Pecorino at the table.

4 tbsp/55 g unsalted butter

¼ cup/40 g pine nuts

6 to 8 large fresh sage leaves

TAGLIARINI WITH ASPARAGUS, MASCARPONE, AND TOASTED HAZELNUTS

SERVES 4 TO 6

FOR THE PASTA DOUGH:

3½ cups/450 g all-purpose flour, plus more for dusting

4 large eggs

Tagliarini is a cut of strand pasta a little wider than capellini, and flat. These are wonderful noodles for dressing in this silky sauce of gently melted mascarpone. The freshness of the asparagus lightens this dish considerably, while the toasted hazelnuts tie it all together beautifully.

TO MAKE THE PASTA DOUGH: Put the flour in a large bowl and make a well in the center. Break the eggs into the center of the well. Using a fork, beat the eggs and begin to pull flour from the sides of the well a little at a time. Gradually add more flour from the well to the mix as you work, until all of the flour is incorporated and a sticky dough forms.

Turn the dough out onto a generously floured work surface and knead, adding more flour as needed to prevent sticking, until the dough is soft and supple, about 5 minutes. Roll the dough into a ball and wrap tightly with plastic wrap. Let rest at room temperature for 1 hour.

Unwrap the dough and cut in half. Return one half to the plastic wrap and keep covered. Cut the other piece of dough in half again. Run one dough piece through a pasta machine with the rollers at the widest setting. Repeat, and then roll the dough twice through each successively narrower setting, until you have a sheet about $\frac{1}{16}$ in/2 mm thick. As you work, dust your hands, the rollers, and the dough lightly with flour as needed to prevent sticking, and lay the finished sheet on a lightly floured work surface. Repeat with the second piece of dough. Attach the cutting blade to the pasta machine and cut the sheets into tagliarini, or $\frac{1}{16}$ in/2 mm wide. Sprinkle the noodles with a small amount of flour to keep them from sticking and spread out on a dry kitchen towel or piece of parchment paper.

TO MAKE THE SAUCE: Bring a large pot of water to a boil and add a small handful of salt. Add the asparagus and cook until tender but still slightly firm to the bite, 3 to 4 minutes.

Remove the pot from the heat. Using a slotted spoon or wire skimmer, transfer the asparagus to a colander; reserve the water to cook the tagliarini later. Immediately place the asparagus under cold running water to stop the cooking, then pat dry on a kitchen towel. Cut the tips and tender tops into 1-in/2.5-cm pieces and finely dice the stems.

Melt the butter in a large sauté pan or skillet over medium heat. Add the asparagus, season with salt and pepper, and sauté for a minute or two, just to warm the asparagus through and get some golden edges. Remove from the heat and add the mascarpone. Set aside.

Meanwhile, return the water to high heat and bring back to a boil. Add the tagliarini and cook, stirring constantly, until al dente, about 45 seconds. Drain the pasta, reserving ½ cup/120 ml of the cooking water, and add to the pan with the asparagus and mascarpone. Add the Parmigiano and stir quickly to melt the mascarpone into a creamy sauce. Add a splash of the reserved pasta cooking water if the pasta seems too dry. Season with more salt and pepper.

Transfer the pasta to a large serving bowl or individual plates. Top with the toasted hazelnuts and serve immediately. Pass more grated Parmigiano at the table.

FOR THE SAUCE:

Sea salt

1 lb/455 g asparagus, tough woody ends removed

2 tbsp unsalted butter

Freshly cracked black pepper

9 oz/255 g mascarpone cheese

6 tbsp/45 g freshly grated Parmigiano-Reggiano cheese, plus more for serving

¾ cup/85 g hazelnuts, toasted and finely chopped

VENETIAN RISOTTO WITH FRESH PEAS AND MONTE VERONESE (RISI E BISI)

SERVES 4 TO 6

1 lb/455 g English peas, in their pods

Sea salt

4 tbsp/55 g unsalted butter, plus 3 tbsp at room temperature for finishing the risotto

1 large shallot, minced

2 cups/400 g Carnaroli or Arborio rice

1 cup/240 ml dry white wine

4 oz/115 g Monte Veronese or Asiago cheese, grated, plus more for serving

Freshly cracked black pepper

This traditional and classic Venetian dish has been well loved the world over, and is one of the best ways to appreciate spring's sugary sweet English peas. The typical chicken stock used in other risotti is replaced here by the water used to poach the peas, carrying their fragrance and flavor all the way to the heart of each perfectly cooked grain of rice.

Monte Veronese is an Asiago-like cow's-milk cheese from the mountains around Verona. It is a fantastic grating cheese, and its nutty flavors pair perfectly with the sweet peas. A younger Asiago would work as well here.

Shell the peas and keep both the peas and their pods, separated. In a large pot, bring 2 qt/2 L water to a boil over high heat. Add the pea pods to the water, reduce the heat to maintain a gentle simmer, and cook for about 15 minutes, or until the water has become a fully flavored pea broth. Strain the broth into a saucepan and discard the cooked pods. Season the pea broth with plenty of salt and keep warm over medium-low heat.

Melt the 4 tbsp/55 g butter in a large sauté pan or skillet over medium heat. Add the shallot and cook until translucent, about 5 minutes. Add the rice all at once and stir, being sure to coat all the grains with the butter. Cook for about 5 minutes, stirring constantly, or until the outside layer of the rice grains becomes translucent. Add the wine and stir constantly until completely absorbed, 2 to 3 minutes longer.

Add the shelled peas and a ladleful of the hot pea broth, stirring constantly. Continue adding the pea broth, one ladleful at a time. As the broth is absorbed, continue adding more, all the while striking a balance between keeping the rice undulating but not swimming in liquid (although this dish is typically served wetter than other regional risotto).

After 15 to 20 minutes, the rice and peas should be cooked, with a nice chew still left in the rice without it being crunchy. Remove from the heat and add the cheese and the remaining 3 tbsp butter, stirring well to create an ultra-creamy risotto. Season with salt and plenty of freshly cracked pepper.

Pour the risotto into a warmed large serving bowl or divide among warmed individual bowls and serve immediately. Pass more grated Monte Veronese at the table.

GRILLED BABY LAMB CHOPS WITH FETA AND ZOGGHIU MINT SAUCE

SERVES 4

FOR THE SAUCE:

1½ cups/45 g loosely packed fresh mint leaves

1½ cups/45 g loosely packed fresh flat-leaf (Italian) parsley leaves

2 small garlic cloves

Sea salt and freshly cracked black pepper

6 tbsp/90 ml extra-virgin olive oil

3 tbsp fresh lemon juice, plus more if needed

16 baby lamb chops

2 tbsp extra-virgin olive oil

Sea salt and freshly cracked black pepper

4 oz/115 g feta cheese, preferably Greek

Some of the finest Greek ruins in the Mediterranean can be found on the magical island of Sicily, in southern Italy. The temple at Segesta is one of the best-preserved examples of Ancient Greek architecture in the world, with thirty-six towering columns still standing against the brutal tests of time. Greeks have been living on the island since around 750 B.C., and their influence is keenly felt in the melting-pot cuisine, language, art, and culture of the land.

In keeping with this influence, I have united the Greek flair for crumbling feta cheese over hot lamb chops with the Sicilian genius of *zogghiu,* a light, fresh, and lively take on pesto made of fresh mint, parsley, garlic, vinegar, and fruity olive oil. The brightness of the *zogghiu,* the salty creaminess of warm feta, and the rich charred flavors of grilled lamb work together in a way that feels nothing short of timeless. While the *zogghiu* can be made quite easily in a food processor, I implore you to go out of your way to prepare it in a mortar and pestle, wherein you will achieve the most brilliant green color and purity of flavors.

TO MAKE THE SAUCE: Combine the mint, parsley, garlic, ½ tsp salt, and a few grindings of pepper in a mortar and crush together with the pestle to form a thick paste. Add the olive oil and continue working the mixture until creamy. Add the lemon juice and stir to mix well. Taste and adjust the seasoning with more lemon juice, or salt and pepper. Set aside.

Build a hot fire in a charcoal grill and let burn until the coals are red hot with a coating of ash, or preheat a gas grill to its highest heat.

Bring the lamb chops to room temperature. Rub the chops with the olive oil and season on both sides with plenty of salt and freshly cracked pepper. Arrange the chops on the grill directly over the heat and grill, turning once, for about 2 minutes on each side for medium-rare. (Cook for 1 to 2 minutes longer if you prefer them medium.)

Transfer the chops to a serving platter. Drizzle the *zogghiu* over the chops while they are still piping hot from the grill, then crumble the feta over the entire dish and serve immediately.

LEMON MASCARPONE TARTS WITH CHOCOLATE-PISTACHIO CRUST

MAKES SIX 5-IN/12-CM INDIVIDUAL TARTS

FOR THE TART DOUGH:

1½ cups/190 g all-purpose flour, plus more for dusting

2 tbsp unsweetened cocoa powder, preferably Dutch process

Pinch of sea salt

7 tbsp/100 g cold unsalted butter, cut into small cubes

½ cup/100 g sugar

1 large egg, beaten

2 tbsp ice water

3½ oz/100 g raw pistachios, chopped

Years ago, in Italy, I ate a bittersweet dark chocolate gelato with tart and zingy lemon sorbetto together on the same cone. It is a match I have loved ever since.

These rich, almost exotic tart shells are fantastic with a variety of other fillings such as vanilla pastry cream and fresh pears. For the lemon mascarpone filling, don't be obsessed with patisserie perfection in presentation. The handmade look creates a nice balance with the sophistication of the cheese tarts.

TO MAKE THE TART DOUGH BY HAND: Sift together the flour, cocoa, and salt into a bowl. Add the butter pieces and toss to coat. Using your hands, work quickly to cut in the butter, rubbing it into the flour mixture with your fingertips until the mixture resembles coarse crumbs, with large pieces of butter still visible. Add the sugar, egg, and ice water to the mixture and stir just to combine. Fold in the pistachios gently. Take care not to work the dough too much, or the crust will be tough.

TO MAKE THE TART DOUGH IN A FOOD PROCESSOR: In the work bowl of a food processor fitted with the blade attachment, combine the flour, cocoa, and salt and pulse to mix. Add the butter pieces and pulse just until a crumbly mixture with butter pieces the size of small peas forms. Add the sugar, egg, and ice water to the mixture and pulse until the dough just comes together. Add the pistachios and pulse a few more times, taking care not to overwork.

Turn the dough out onto a well-floured work surface and gently form it into a ball. Wrap the dough in plastic wrap and refrigerate for at least 1 hour, or up to 24 hours.

Preheat the oven to 350°F/180°C.

Unwrap the dough and roll it out on a lightly floured work surface into a rough rectangle about ⅛ in/3 mm thick. (If the dough is too stiff to roll out, let stand for a few minutes to loosen up.) Cut the dough into six equal pieces and gently press each piece into a 5-in/12-cm tart mold with a removable bottom, pressing it into the corners and trimming any excess. If the dough tears here and there, no worries; simply press the dough into the mold evenly using the tips of your fingers.

Arrange the tart shells on a baking sheet, prick the bottoms all over with a fork and refrigerate for 10 minutes, then line with parchment paper and fill with dried beans or pie weights. Bake for 10 to 15 minutes, or until the edges are firm. Remove the paper and beans and bake for 3 to 5 minutes longer, or until the bottoms of the shells are firm and dry but not browned. Remove from the oven and let cool completely before gently removing from the molds.

TO MAKE THE FILLING: In a bowl, combine the mascarpone, sugar, and lemon juice and zest and stir gently with a spoon until smooth.

Divide the filling among the cooled tart shells and spread smooth with the back of a small spoon or inverted spatula. Garnish with a light sprinkling of cocoa powder, a sprinkling of pistachios, and fresh raspberries, if you like. Refrigerate the tarts until well chilled, at least 1 hour and up to 3 hours, before serving.

FOR THE FILLING:

1 lb/455 g good-quality mascarpone cheese, at room temperature

½ cup/100 g sugar

Juice and zest of 2 lemons

Cocoa powder for garnish

Chopped pistachios for garnish

18 ripe raspberries for garnish (optional)

SUMMER

Charentais Melon with Serrano Ham and Garroxta 52

Watermelon with Pecorino Stravecchio and
White Balsamic Vinegar 54

Black Mission Figs and Fresh Robiola with
White Truffle Oil Wrapped in Bresaola 55

White Figs with Pecorino Sardo and Mugolio Pine Syrup 56

Savory Fig and Gouda Cake 58

Bocconcini di Pura Capra Toasts with Blackberries and Honey 59

Buttermilk Biscuit Sandwiches with Homemade Blackberry Jam,
Smoked Ham, and Pondhopper Goat Cheese 60

Strawberry and Fresh Thyme Jam for Goat Cheeses 62

Strawberry Risotto with Fresh Robiola 64

Roasted Beets and Fresh Strawberries
with Orange Syrup and Goat Cheese 66

Bing Cherry and Goat-Cheese Pudding 69

Black Cherry Mostarda 70

Challerhocker Sandwiches with
Roasted Apricot–Rosemary Mustard 72

Apricot–Olive Oil Tea Cakes with Ricotta and Pistachios 74

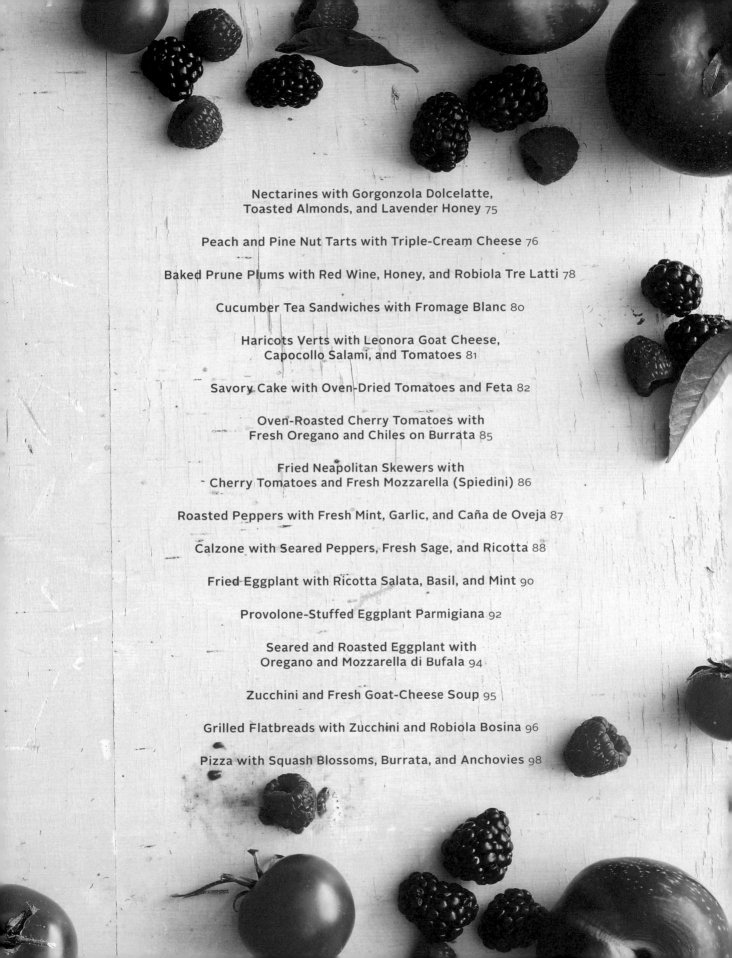

Nectarines with Gorgonzola Dolcelatte,
Toasted Almonds, and Lavender Honey 75

Peach and Pine Nut Tarts with Triple-Cream Cheese 76

Baked Prune Plums with Red Wine, Honey, and Robiola Tre Latti 78

Cucumber Tea Sandwiches with Fromage Blanc 80

Haricots Verts with Leonora Goat Cheese,
Capocollo Salami, and Tomatoes 81

Savory Cake with Oven-Dried Tomatoes and Feta 82

Oven-Roasted Cherry Tomatoes with
Fresh Oregano and Chiles on Burrata 85

Fried Neapolitan Skewers with
Cherry Tomatoes and Fresh Mozzarella (Spiedini) 86

Roasted Peppers with Fresh Mint, Garlic, and Caña de Oveja 87

Calzone with Seared Peppers, Fresh Sage, and Ricotta 88

Fried Eggplant with Ricotta Salata, Basil, and Mint 90

Provolone-Stuffed Eggplant Parmigiana 92

Seared and Roasted Eggplant with
Oregano and Mozzarella di Bufala 94

Zucchini and Fresh Goat-Cheese Soup 95

Grilled Flatbreads with Zucchini and Robiola Bosina 96

Pizza with Squash Blossoms, Burrata, and Anchovies 98

CHARENTAIS MELON WITH SERRANO HAM AND GARROXTA

SERVES 8 TO 10

1 small Charentais melon

1 tbsp finely chopped fresh mint

9 oz/255 g Garroxta or other semihard goat cheese

4 to 5 oz/115 to 140 g Serrano ham, thinly sliced

Charentais melons originally come from the Poitou-Charentes region of France, but the variety has become popular for growing throughout similar climates worldwide. Smaller than cantaloupe, Charentais are packed with a mind-blowing fragrance and dense, honey-like sweetness that go perfectly with rich serrano ham and salty aged goat cheese.

It is said that Garroxta (pronounced gar-roe-cha) is made from the milk of goats that graze on a heavy diet of wild herbs in the mountains of Catalonia, thus imparting very apparent herbal notes to the cheese. Similar in texture to many pecorino cheeses, Garroxta's raw-goat-milk flavor pairs amazingly with cured meats and salami.

The salts from both the ham and the cheese tend to draw out the juices of the melon, so it is best to prepare all of the components in advance and then prepare the completed dish right before serving, or present this dish deconstructed, beautifully arranged on a platter, and instruct your guest to assemble their own bites.

Cut a thin slice off each end of the melon with a sharp knife. Stand the melon upright on a cutting board. Cut from the top-side down to remove the rind in sections, working all the way around and following the contour of the fruit, until all the rind is removed. Cut the melon in half lengthwise and scoop out the seeds with a spoon. Discard the seeds and rind.

Cut each half of the melon lengthwise into eight thin wedges, then cut the wedges in half crosswise for a total of 32 pieces. Put the slices in a bowl and toss with the mint.

Cut the rind off the cheese and cut into 32 equal slices. Place a slice of cheese on a slice of melon, then wrap with a piece of ham. Repeat to assemble all the bundles. (You can make neat bundles hiding the melon and cheese, although I prefer a rustic look, with a bit of all the ingredients poking out.)

Serve on a platter with small wooden skewers or toothpicks.

WATERMELON WITH PECORINO STRAVECCHIO AND WHITE BALSAMIC VINEGAR

SERVES 4 TO 6

One 1-lb/455-g chunk ripe watermelon

2 oz/55 g Pecorino Stravecchio or other aged sheep's-milk cheese

1 tsp white balsamic vinegar

1 tsp thinly sliced fresh mint

Freshly cracked black pepper

Watermelon and balsamic vinegar together are one of the truly great pairings, and the flavors that linger from the union of just these two components alone are delightful. Add the nutty, salty flavors of aged sheep's-milk cheese, a light kick from freshly cracked black pepper, and just a whisper of fresh mint, and you have a salad that is not only powerful in its austerity, but a bright and beautiful opening to a meal or the perfect surprise to cleanse the palate between the main course and dessert.

This salad is best prepped in advance and then composed at the last minute. I enjoy the smaller watermelons to the large beasts of my childhood, and there will be less left over using them. Use your imagination as to the shapes and sizes of the cut fruit and cheese, but while melon balls and shaved pecorino are a pretty way to go, the flavors are more balanced if the cheese is cut into slightly thicker pieces.

If white balsamic vinegar is unavailable, traditional balsamic vinegar will work wonderfully, but will make a darker presentation. Also, a good-quality Banyuls vinegar is perfect with this combination.

Remove the rind from the watermelon and cut the flesh into ½-in/12-mm cubes, or use a small melon baller to make same-size balls. Place the watermelon in a medium bowl.

Cut the Pecorino into ¼-in/6-mm cubes, or break it into rougher chunks about half the size of the watermelon pieces. Add the cheese to the watermelon and toss with the vinegar, mint, and a few grindings of pepper. Divide among individual plates or cordial glasses and serve immediately.

I am opposed to the abuse truffle oil has suffered of late, how it is too often forced into the strangest dishes in an attempt to conjure flavor and sophistication where there is an absence of both. Still, it has its place and its purpose, and serves well, even stunningly, if used judiciously. This, in my humble opinion, is such an application—where the perfume of white truffle not only shines as the star it is, but also works in harmony with the other heavenly ingredients.

Robiola Osella is a fluffy, tangy-sweet cow's-milk cheese from Piedmonte. It is as indispensable in the kitchen as it is on the cheese board, and can be found more and more readily in fine food stores, cheese shops, and online.

Bresaola is a rich, slightly gamey air-cured beef tenderloin that has been salted and aged for two to three months. Originally from northern Italy's Valtellina region, bresaola is now being artisanally produced outside of Italy; a particularly nice version comes from Uruguay. Like prosciutto, bresaola is most often sliced paper-thin.

Cut the figs in half lengthwise and lay out on a clean work surface, cut-side up.

Slice the cheese into 16 equal pieces and place one atop each fig half. With your thumb over the bottle opening, drop a single bead of truffle oil onto the cheese, then wrap each assembled bite with a piece of bresaola. Arrange the wrapped figs attractively on a serving platter as you work. Serve immediately, at room temperature.

BLACK MISSION FIGS AND FRESH ROBIOLA WITH WHITE TRUFFLE OIL WRAPPED IN BRESAOLA

SERVES 4

8 ripe large black Mission figs, stemmed

6 oz/170 g Robiola Osella cheese

White truffle oil for drizzling

16 thin slices bresaola

WHITE FIGS WITH PECORINO SARDO AND MUGOLIO PINE SYRUP

SERVES 4

8 ripe medium white or green figs, stemmed

2 oz/55 g Pecorino Sardo or other aged sheep's-milk cheese

16 drops Mugolio pine bud syrup or chestnut honey

Deep in the Dolomite Mountains of northern Italy, a woman by the name of Eleanora Cuancia handpicks the springtime buds of Mugolio pine trees, puts them in glass jars, and lets them bake in the sun for several months. During that time, the baby pine cones release a perfumed sap that Signora Cuancia cooks down with sugar over a wood fire, reducing the mixture to a caramel-colored syrup with a fragrance of the wild woods.

Mugolio pine syrup can be purchased in small bottles from several online sources and in fine cheese shops. A little goes a very long way. A single drop on a mouthful of aged pecorino and ripe figs is a lesson in simplicity and elegance. Dark honey, such as chestnut or buckwheat, would be a fine substitute, but I encourage you to find a bottle of this magical elixir and keep it stored in a dark cool place for those special guests you really want to wow! Mugolio is equally delightful atop plain vanilla ice cream with a sprinkle of toasted sesame seeds or brushed on roasted duck. I have even heard of martinis being mixed with a bead of Mugolio.

You can cut the figs and arrange the cheese atop them ahead of time, but it is best to drizzle the pine syrup or honey at the last minute before serving. In fact, Mugolio is such a treasure, I love to drip the syrup on the figs and cheese right in front of my guests.

Cut the figs in half lengthwise and arrange on a serving dish, cut-side up.

Slice the cheese into 16 equal pieces and place one atop each fig half. With your thumb over the bottle opening, drop a single bead of Mugolio pine syrup onto the cheese. If using honey, dip the tines of a fork into the honey and drizzle a small thread over the cheese. Serve immediately, at room temperature.

SAVORY FIG AND GOUDA CAKE

MAKES ONE 4½-BY-10-IN/11-BY-25-CM
LOAF CAKE; SERVES 6 TO 8

2 cups/255 g all-purpose flour

1 tbsp baking powder

1 tsp sea salt

Freshly cracked black pepper

3 large eggs

½ cup/120 ml extra-virgin olive oil

½ cup/120 ml whole milk

7 oz/200 g ripe medium black figs,
stemmed and halved

5 oz/140 g goat's-milk Gouda, shredded

Savory cakes are a French phenomenon that somehow have yet to catch on in the States. Served with pre-dinner drinks or added to a picnic basket, they are a quintessentially homemade dish, often the result of a creative raid of the icebox. The base is pretty much standard, but the endless variety of cheese, salami, olives, vegetables, and fruits to add is astounding.

This particular combination of sweet figs and tangy goat's-milk Gouda makes a wonderful appetizer or can be the foundation of a picnic. Cut the cake into small squares and serve it with a few slices of prosciutto or salami and a crisp green salad.

Preheat the oven to 350°F/180°C. Line a 4½-by-10-in/11-by-25-cm loaf pan with parchment paper, using two pieces if necessary to cover both the bottom and the sides.

In a large bowl, whisk together the flour, baking powder, salt, and a few grindings of pepper. In a medium bowl, whisk together the eggs, olive oil, and milk until well combined.

Slowly whisk the egg mixture into the flour mixture, then switch to a wooden spoon and stir until a thick, smooth batter is formed. Add the figs and cheese, reserving a few tablespoons of the cheese to sprinkle on top, and stir until just mixed.

Pour the batter into the prepared pan, making sure the figs are evenly distributed. Sprinkle the reserved cheese over the top and bake for 45 to 50 minutes, or until a wooden skewer inserted into the middle of the cake comes out clean.

Remove the cake from the oven and let it cool in the pan on a wire rack for 10 minutes, then turn the cake out onto the rack and let it cool completely. Cut into thick slices and serve. Leftover cake can be wrapped in plastic wrap and stored in the refrigerator for up to 3 days and is best brought back to room temperature before enjoying again.

I read about this combination in one of those wonderful food magazines you find at the train stations in France, and had to try it. Sure enough: heaven! Serve alone or with a handful of mixed greens and edible wildflowers dressed with a good extra-virgin olive oil.

Bocconcini di Pura Capra are not the fresh mozzarella balls typically found by the name of *bocconcini,* but rather light and airy soft-ripened goat's-milk discs from Piedmonte, Italy. Rocamadour, Cabecou, or even slices of ripe Brie would all work well, too.

Preheat the broiler.

In a small bowl, combine the blackberries, honey, thyme, and a grinding of pepper. Stir with a fork to mix well, mashing the berries but leaving some nice chunks intact.

Arrange the bread slices on a baking sheet. Place under the broiler until the tops are golden, about 1 minute. Turn and lightly toast on the second side, about 30 seconds longer. Watch carefully to avoid burning. Remove immediately. Leave the broiler on.

Spread about 1 tbsp of the blackberry mixture on each slice of toasted bread, then place a cheese half atop the blackberry mixture on each toast.

Return the toasts to the broiler for 1 to 2 minutes, until the cheese is warmed through and slightly golden on the edges. Serve immediately.

BOCCONCINI DI PURA CAPRA TOASTS WITH BLACKBERRIES AND HONEY

SERVES 4

4 oz/115 g ripe blackberries

1 tbsp wildflower honey

Leaves of 2 fresh thyme sprigs, finely chopped

Freshly cracked black pepper

8 slices whole-grain or seeded baguette, each about ½ in/12 mm thick

4 Bocconcini di Pura Capra, Rocamadour, or other small disks of soft-ripened goat cheese, cut in half horizontally

BUTTERMILK BISCUIT SANDWICHES WITH HOMEMADE BLACKBERRY JAM, SMOKED HAM, AND PONDHOPPER GOAT CHEESE

MAKES 16 BISCUIT SANDWICHES

FOR THE BISCUITS:

1 large egg

1¼ cups/300 ml buttermilk

1½ cups/190 g cups all-purpose flour

1½ cups/150 g cake flour

¼ cup/50 g sugar

I cannot say enough about the blackberry bush. Those beautiful brambles were the first real success I had in the garden. While that may not be any real great achievement, due to the fortitude of the plant, I was encouraged to keep gardening. The blackberry bush has also given me countless hours of enjoyment with my children. One early May, my son and I went out to the garden to collect what we thought would be a nice handful of ripe-and-ready berries. We ended up with a large basketful! And there were still more to come.

Picked right from the bush, still warm from the sun, the blackberry's flavor is dizzying. We raced into the kitchen, weighed our take, rinsed it, and tossed the berries in a saucepan with sugar and a few squeezes of lemon from the tree out back. Fifteen minutes later, the jam was done. We spooned it into sterilized jars and set about making the labels. There may be no finer gift to give than homemade handpicked blackberry jam, and while there are incredible jams available made by artisans the world over, the easy recipe here is likely to be a revelation. This recipe makes about 1 cup/360 g of jam, but you can double, triple, or even quadruple the ingredients and preserve the jam in jars to keep for yourself or to give away as gifts (see Strawberry and Fresh Thyme Jam for Goat Cheeses on page 62 for canning instructions).

Pondhopper is a semisoft goat cheese from Oregon. Sharp, tangy, and creamy, it's a phenomenal sandwich cheese. A goat's-milk Gouda or sharp cow's-milk Cheddar would work nicely as well.

And the biscuits? Well, they're a Sunday morning staple in my house with blackberry jam or wild honey. They can also be split in half and covered with fresh strawberries tossed in sugar along with a dollop of vanilla bean ice cream for fantastic summer dessert.

TO MAKE THE BISCUITS: Position a rack in the upper third of the oven and preheat to 475°F/240°C. Line a baking sheet with parchment paper.

In a large bowl, whisk together the egg and buttermilk. Set aside.

Sift together both flours, the sugar, baking powder, cream of tartar, and salt into a medium bowl. Add the butter pieces and toss to coat. Using your hands, work quickly to cut in the butter, rubbing it into the flour mixture with your fingertips until the mixture resembles coarse crumbs, with large pieces of butter still visible.

Add the egg mixture to the flour mixture and stir quickly with a wooden spoon just until a very loose, ragged dough forms. Take care not to overmix, or the biscuits will be tough. Turn the dough out onto a well-floured work surface. Dust your hands with flour, too, and gently pat the dough into an 8-in/20-cm square about 1½ in/4 cm thick. Using a sharp knife, cut the square into sixteen 2-in/5-cm biscuits.

Transfer the biscuits to the prepared baking sheet, allowing as much space between them as possible. Bake in the upper part of the oven until puffed and golden, 12 to 15 minutes. Remove from the heat and let cool slightly.

WHILE THE BISCUITS ARE BAKING, MAKE THE JAM: Quickly rinse and drain the blackberries, then put them in a large nonreactive saucepan. Add the sugar and lemon juice and stir to combine. Place over medium heat and cook, stirring often with a wooden spoon, until the sugar is melted and the blackberries begin releasing their juices, about 5 minutes.

Raise the heat to medium-high and cook, stirring constantly, until the jam has thickened and coats the back of a chilled metal spoon, about 15 minutes longer.

To assemble the sandwiches, cut the biscuits in half horizontally. Spread a rounded 1 tsp jam on each biscuit half. (Spread a little more thickly, if you like; you should have ample jam.) Place one slice of the cheese on the bottom half of each biscuit, followed by a slice of ham, folding it as needed to fit. Replace the biscuit tops and serve immediately.

2 tsp baking powder

½ tsp cream of tartar

½ tsp sea salt

½ cup/115 g cold unsalted butter, cut into small cubes

FOR THE BLACKBERRY JAM:

1 lb/455 g ripe blackberries

1 cup/200 g sugar

2 tbsp fresh lemon juice

6 oz/170 g Pondhopper cheese or other sharp aged cheese, cut into 16 slices

1 lb/455 g Virginia ham or other high-quality smoked ham, thickly sliced

STRAWBERRY AND FRESH THYME JAM FOR GOAT CHEESES

MAKES ABOUT 4 CUPS/910 G

2 lb/910 g ripe strawberries, hulled and roughly chopped

2 cups/680 g mild honey

12 fresh thyme sprigs

Juice of 1 lemon

I know that strawberries are in peak season when I'm walking through the farmers' market and, like the old Merrie Melodies cartoons, that unmistakable fragrance reaches into my nostrils like two phantom fingers, lifting me off my feet and leading me floating toward the bright red bounty.

Bright, fresh strawberries cooked down with the earthy fragrance of fresh thyme from the garden is a delight atop goat's- and sheep's-milk cheeses. I particularly love this jam with slabs of Nevat, a creamy, dense soft-ripened goat cheese from Catalonia. This simple jam, made "not too sweet" by using honey instead of sugar, is a splendid gift for friends and family.

If you don't want to can this jam for longer storing, just can for the short term: Remove the jam from the heat and let cool slightly, then transfer to clean glass jars or other containers with airtight lids. Let cool completely before covering tightly. Refrigerate for up to 1 month.

Have ready four clean ½-pt/225-g canning jars with new lids and rings.

In a large bowl, combine the strawberries, honey, and thyme and stir well. Let the mixture sit for 15 minutes, or until the honey has dissolved and the strawberries have begun to release their juices. Stir in the lemon juice and transfer the mixture to a large, nonreactive sauce pan, being sure not to leave behind any of the juices.

Bring the mixture to a bubble over medium heat, stirring often. When the jam begins to bubble, raise the heat to high and continue to cook over high heat for 8 to 12 minutes, until the jam is thick and sticky and coats the back of a chilled metal spoon, about 15 minutes longer.

While the jam is cooking, fill a canner fitted with a jar rack or a pot fitted with a steamer rack about halfway full of water and place over high heat. Bring a teakettle of water to a boil at the same time. Wash the jar lids and rings in hot soapy water; rinse thoroughly and put in a bowl of hot water. When the pot of water is hot but not boiling yet, using tongs or a jar lifter, lower the canning jars into the hot water and settle them on the rack. Add more hot water from the teakettle if needed to cover the jars by about 1 in/2.5 cm. Bring the water to a full boil, then adjust the heat for a gentle boil and boil the jars for 10 minutes to sterilize. Using the tongs, transfer to a clean kitchen towel. Reduce the water temperature to a bare simmer.

Using a deep soupspoon or small ladle, spoon the hot jam into the sterilized jars, preferably while the jars are still hot. Leave a ¼-in/6-mm headspace at the top (but no more than that, or excess air may cause spoilage). Use a damp towel to clean any drips off the rims of the jars. Place the lids on the jars, using the end of a spoon or a chopstick (or a magnet stick, if you have one) to nudge them out of the hot water, and handling them only by the edges. Screw on the rims firmly (but not as tight as possible). Use the tongs to lower the filled jars back into the rack. Raise the heat to achieve a full but gentle boil again, then cover and begin timing; boil for 5 minutes. Remove the jars and let cool completely. Store the jam in a cool, dark place for up to 6 months. Refrigerate after opening.

STRAWBERRY RISOTTO WITH FRESH ROBIOLA

SERVES 4 TO 6

6 cups/1.4 L chicken stock, homemade or good-quality low-sodium purchased

4 tbsp/55 g unsalted butter

1 medium shallot, minced

2 cups/400 g Carnaroli or Arborio rice

1 cup/240 ml Prosecco

12 oz/340 g ripe but firm strawberries, hulled and thinly sliced

3½ oz/100 g fresh Robiola cheese

2 oz/55 g Parmigiano-Reggiano cheese, grated

Sea salt and freshly cracked black pepper

This is one of those dishes that always gets an "ooh" whenever it is mentioned. Warm, fragrant strawberries that stain the rice a romantic pink are balanced with the rich creamy Robiola used in place of the traditional butter at the end. If you can find the sweet cubes of cow's-milk Robiola Osella, fantastic. Otherwise, the Tre Latti (sheep-cow-goat) or all goat's-milk varieties of Robiola will work nicely as well.

Risotto tends to feel more appropriate in the cooler months, but this is a great way to exploit the very best strawberries in the heat of summer. It pairs beautifully with grilled birds like quail, or could be the focus of a meal in itself, followed by a crisp salad.

In a saucepan, warm the stock over medium heat until hot. Reduce the heat to medium-low and keep the pan on a nearby burner while you cook the risotto.

Melt the butter in a large sauté pan over medium heat. Add the shallot and cook until translucent, about 5 minutes. Add the rice all at once and stir, being sure to coat all the grains with the butter. Cook for about 5 minutes, stirring constantly, or until the outside layer of the rice grains becomes translucent. Add the Prosecco and stir constantly until completely absorbed, 2 to 3 minutes longer.

Begin adding the hot stock, one ladleful at a time, stirring constantly. As the stock is absorbed, continue adding more, all the while striking a balance between keeping the rice undulating but not swimming in liquid.

After 15 or 20 minutes, the rice should be cooked, with a nice chew but not crunchy. Stir in the strawberries and cook for 1 minute longer, then remove from the heat and add the Robiola and Parmigiano, stirring well to combine the cheeses and create an ultra-creamy risotto. Season with salt and plenty of freshly cracked pepper. Serve immediately.

ROASTED BEETS AND FRESH STRAW-BERRIES WITH ORANGE SYRUP AND GOAT CHEESE

SERVES 4 TO 6

1 lb/455 g small beets, scrubbed but not peeled, tops trimmed to about 1 in/2.5 cm

4 tbsp/60 ml extra-virgin olive oil

⅓ cup/75 ml fresh mandarin or orange juice

2 oz/55 g lamb's lettuce (mâche) or watercress

Freshly cracked black pepper

6 oz/170 g ripe strawberries, hulled and cut into slices about ¼ in/6 mm thick

4 oz/115 g fresh soft-ripened goat cheese

Fresh untreated lavender flowers for garnish (optional)

I first experienced the combination of beets and straw-berries at the magical Blackberry Farm in the Great Smoky Mountains of Tennessee, in a simple salad of pickled beets and ripe strawberries straight from their prolific garden. This coupling makes a wonderful marriage of flavors, and is a visual delight.

The perfume of strawberries and the deep earthy flavors of beets are combined here with a reduction of mandarin orange juice and extra-virgin olive oil. The creamy goat cheese against these bright flavors unites the dish.

Although many fresh goat's-milk cheeses would work here, I prefer a soft-ripened goat cheese such as Tomme de Ma Grand-Mère from the Loire Valley, with its velvety texture and clean, tart flavors. Humboldt Fog from Northern California or the great Spanish Caña de Cabra would also work wonders.

Preheat the oven to 425°F/220°C.

Put the beets in a small roasting pan, drizzle with 1 tbsp of the olive oil, and toss to coat. Roast for 1 hour, or until a knife pierces through to the center easily. Remove from the oven and let cool to room temperature, then slip the skins off with your fingers, using the tip of a paring knife to help loosen them, if needed. (I don't mind the stain of beets on my hands—proof that I've been cooking for my family!—but you may want to wear kitchen gloves to prevent stains.) Cut each beet into eight wedges and set aside.

While the beets are roasting, pour the mandarin juice into a small saucepan and bring to a boil over high heat. Reduce the heat to medium-low and simmer for 10 to 15 minutes, or until the juice is reduced by half and a nice, thick syrup has formed. Pour into a medium bowl and set aside to cool to room temperature.

To assemble the salad, in a large bowl, toss the lamb's lettuce with 1 tbsp of the olive oil until evenly coated. Divide among individual plates or bowls. Whisk the remaining 2 tbsp olive oil into the orange syrup and season with pepper. (Reserve a few drops of the orange syrup to decorate the plates, if you like.)

cont'd

Add the strawberries and beets to the dressing and stir gently to coat and mix well, then divide among the salads. Crumble the goat cheese over each serving, dividing it evenly, and drizzle any remaining juices from the dressed beets and straw- berries over the salad. Add a few drops of any left- over orange syrup and some tiny lavender flowers, if desired, for a stunning effect. Serve immediately.

This cherry pudding, based on a classic clafoutis, the famous custard (or more like pan pudding) from Limousin, France, takes on a little zing with the addition of fresh goat cheese. The sweet, warm fruit against the earthy, dense goat cheese is a lesson in balance of both flavor and texture. Serve this dessert for a dramatic finish to a late-summer meal—you can even serve it straight from the pan in the center of the table. Just pass out some nice silver spoons and let everyone dig in.

Combine the goat cheese and the ½ cup/100 g granulated sugar in a bowl. Using an electric mixer set on low speed, beat until smooth, about 2 minutes. Add the eggs, one at a time, beating until each one is incorporated before adding the next. Add the honey, cream, and vanilla and beat until just combined. Sift in the flour and beat just until no lumps remain. Cover the bowl and let the batter rest at room temperature for 1 hour.

Preheat the oven to 350°F/180°C. Grease a 10-in/25-cm square baking dish with the butter.

Using a rubber spatula, scrape the batter into the prepared baking dish and spread the surface smooth. In a bowl, toss the cherries with the 2 tbsp granulated sugar. Arrange the cherries evenly over the surface of the batter.

Bake for 30 to 40 minutes, or until the top is golden brown and a toothpick inserted into the center comes out clean. Remove from the oven and let cool and settle for at least 20 minutes before serving. Serve warm or at room temperature, dusted with confectioners' sugar.

BING CHERRY AND GOAT-CHEESE PUDDING

MAKES ONE 10-IN/25-CM PUDDING;
SERVES 6

6 oz/170 g mild goat cheese, at room temperature

½ cup/100 g granulated sugar, plus 2 tbsp

4 large eggs

3 tbsp honey

¾ cup/180 ml heavy (whipping) cream

1 tsp vanilla extract

½ cup/65 g all-purpose flour

1 tbsp unsalted butter, at room temperature

1 lb/455 g fresh Bing cherries, pitted

Confectioners' sugar for dusting

BLACK CHERRY MOSTARDA

MAKES 2 PINTS/910 G

2 lb/910 g dark cherries such as Bing, Sweetheart, or Lambert, pitted

Juice of 1 lemon

2¼ cups/450 g sugar

6 tbsp/45 g dry mustard

6 tbsp/90 ml good-quality balsamic vinegar

Sweet and tart ripe black cherries are a wonderful accompaniment to savory foods, from ultra-rich goat cheese, aged pecorinos, and gooey ripe gorgonzola to gamey roasted birds and sausages. When featured in the Italian fruit-and-mustard chutney known as *mostarda,* these qualities are even more pronounced, especially with the use of good-quality balsamic vinegar, which helps to push the natural cherry flavors forward.

Put the cherries in a large stainless-steel or ceramic bowl. Sprinkle the lemon juice over the cherries, then scatter the sugar over them and stir once. Let rest and macerate at room temperature for 24 hours. Most of the sugar should be dissolved.

Strain the juice and sugar from the cherries into a medium saucepan. Bring to a boil over medium-high heat and cook until the liquid has reduced and a nice, thick syrup has formed, 10 to 15 minutes.

Meanwhile, in a small bowl, whisk together the dry mustard and balsamic vinegar until smooth. Have ready four clean ½-pt/225-g canning jars with new lids and rings.

Fill a canner fitted with a jar rack or a pot fitted with a steamer rack about halfway full of water and place over high heat. Bring a teakettle of water to a boil at the same time. Wash the jar lids and rings in hot soapy water; rinse thoroughly and put in a bowl of hot water. When the pot of water is hot but not boiling yet, using tongs or a jar lifter, lower the canning jars into the hot water and settle them on the rack. Add more hot water from the teakettle if needed to cover the jars by about 1 in/2.5 cm. Bring the water to a full boil, then adjust the heat for a gentle boil and boil the jars for 10 minutes to sterilize. Using the tongs, transfer to a clean kitchen towel. Reduce the water temperature to a bare simmer.

Add the macerated cherries to the cherry syrup and remove from the heat. Pour the mustard mixture into the cherries and stir to combine. Let the mixture cool slightly, then transfer to a food processor fitted with the blade attachment. Process to a coarse purée. (Take good care when processing the cherries to watch for and discard any pits that you may have overlooked.)

Using a deep soupspoon or small ladle, spoon the warm mostarda into the sterilized jars, preferably while the jars are still hot. Leave a ¼-in/6-mm headspace at the top (but no more than that, or excess air may cause spoilage). Use a damp towel to clean any drips off the rims of the jars. Place the lids on the jars, using the end of a spoon or a chopstick (or a magnet stick, if you have one) to nudge them out of the hot water, and handling them only by the edges. Screw on the rims firmly (but not as tight as possible). Use the tongs to lower the filled jars back into the rack. Raise the heat to achieve a full but gentle boil again, then cover and begin timing; boil for 5 minutes. Remove the jars and let cool completely. Store the mostarda in a cool, dark place for up to 6 months. Refrigerate after opening.

CHALLERHOCKER SANDWICHES WITH ROASTED APRICOT—ROSEMARY MUSTARD

SERVES 4

4 ripe apricots, halved and pitted

1 tbsp extra-virgin olive oil

1 tbsp sugar, plus more if needed

½ cup/115 g Dijon or other strong mustard

1 tsp finely chopped fresh rosemary

1 baguette

8 oz/225 g Challerhocker or aged Gruyère de Comté cheese

For me, no other cheese has more mystery and depth of flavor than Challerhocker. This washed-rind cow's-milk cheese from legendary cheesemaker Walter Rass is aged for a minimum of 10 months. Its intriguing name means "the one in the cellar," and with the slightly creepy drawing of a wicked little boy on the label, the mystery deepens. Dense, rich flavors of Alpine milk abound, and the texture resembles a delicate salt caramel.

For my good friends at Oldfield's Liquor Room in Los Angeles, I recently designed a crusty baguette sandwich with a few thick slabs of Challerhocker, a dollop of apricot mustard, and a pinch of fresh rosemary. It's a great snack to keep the appetite whetted for their amazing cocktails.

Aged Gruyère or a really good aged Cheddar works nicely as well. If fresh apricots are not available, using a very high-quality, not-too-sweet apricot jam is a great way to enjoy this sandwich year-round. I like to wrap the sandwiches up in parchment paper for taking on picnics or pile them high on a vintage cake stand for guests to grab.

Preheat the oven to 400°F/200°C.

In a bowl, toss the apricot halves with the olive oil and sugar. Spread the apricot halves out on a baking sheet, cut-sides up. Roast for 25 to 30 minutes, or until the juices are caramelized on the pan and the flesh is very tender.

Transfer the roasted apricots to a medium bowl, along with any of the juices and sugars that aren't too burnt. Mash into a smooth pulp with a fork and let cool completely. Add the mustard and rosemary and stir to mix well. Taste and add a pinch or two more sugar, if needed. The mixture should taste both sweet and spicy.

Cut the baguette in half horizontally and spread both of the cut sides with the apricot-rosemary mustard. Slice the cheese into pieces about ¼ in/6 mm thick and arrange evenly on the bottom half of the baguette. Replace the top half of the baguette, cut into four sandwiches, and serve.

APRICOT–OLIVE OIL TEA CAKES WITH RICOTTA AND PISTACHIOS

MAKES 12 TEA CAKES

1 tsp extra-virgin olive oil, plus 6 tbsp/90 ml

Cake flour (not self-rising) for dusting, plus 1½ cups/185 g

2 tsp baking powder

½ tsp sea salt

2 large eggs

⅔ cup/130 g granulated sugar

Zest of 1 lemon

1 cup/255 g fresh ricotta cheese, drained

3 ripe apricots, halved, pitted, and roughly chopped

½ cup/55 g raw pistachios, coarsely ground

Confectioners' sugar for dusting

These little gems are a perfect afternoon treat with a cup of tea or coffee. Fresh ricotta adds creamy moisture to the crumb of this gloriously simple olive oil cake, perfumed with fruity extra-virgin oil and lemon zest. The tart chunks of fresh apricot provide a delightful tang, with pistachios adding just the right balance to the texture.

Keep in mind that when grinding nuts in a food processor or spice grinder, it's a good idea to pulse in small bursts, so as not to make a nut butter.

I like to make this recipe with pluots (a plum and apricot hybrid) when they are available, as well as plums, nectarines, peaches, and all kinds of berries.

Preheat the oven to 350°F/180°C. Grease a standard 12-cup muffin tin with the 1 tsp olive oil, then dust with flour and tap out any excess (or line the cups with cupcake papers).

In a medium bowl, sift together the 1½ cups/185 g flour, baking powder, and salt. Set aside. In a large bowl, combine the eggs, granulated sugar, 6 tbsp/90 ml olive oil, and lemon zest. Using an electric mixer set on medium speed, beat until the mixture is thick and pale yellow.

Reduce the speed to low and add the ricotta, one large spoonful at a time, beating until just combined after each addition. Add the flour mixture in two or three increments, beating each just until incorporated and the batter is smooth. Using a rubber spatula, fold in the apricots and pistachios.

Divide the batter evenly among the prepared muffin cups, filling them almost to the top. Bake for 20 to 25 minutes, or until a wooden skewer inserted into the center of a cake comes out clean.

Transfer to a wire rack and let cool slightly, then loosen the edges of the cakes with an offset spatula or a thin-bladed knife. Turn the cakes out onto the rack and let cool to room temperature.

Dust lightly with confectioners' sugar and serve. Store the cakes in an airtight container at room temperature for up to 2 days.

Lavender honey has to be one of the most elegant items in my larder, and while I enjoy a spoonful in my Yorkshire tea, it is stunningly suited for drizzling over blue cheeses, particularly creamy Gorgonzola Dolcelatte. This milder version of the famous Gorgonzola blue cheese from northern Italy was developed for the English market, but has become an Italian classic, especially in the kitchen where its extra-creamy texture is prized by chefs.

This is a magical dessert following a summer meal—the combination of flavors sings with harmony and makes me close my eyes in pleasure with every bite.

Halve the nectarines and remove the stones. Cut each half into six slices.

Divide the nectarine slices among individual plates. Crumble the Gorgonzola and scatter it over the nectarine slices. Sprinkle the toasted almonds over the nectarines and cheese, then drizzle the honey all over each portion. Garnish with lavender flowers, if desired, and serve immediately.

NECTARINES WITH GORGONZOLA DOLCELATTE, TOASTED ALMONDS, AND LAVENDER HONEY

SERVES 4

2 large ripe nectarines

2 oz/55 g Gorgonzola Dolcelatte or other creamy blue cheese

2 oz/55 g sliced almonds, lightly toasted

1 tbsp lavender honey

Lavender flowers for garnish (optional)

PEACH AND PINE NUT TARTS WITH TRIPLE-CREAM CHEESE

MAKES SIX 5-IN/12-CM INDIVIDUAL TARTS

FOR THE TART DOUGH:

2 cups/255 g all-purpose flour

⅓ cup/65 g sugar

¼ tsp sea salt

Zest of 1 lemon

¾ cup/170 g cold unsalted butter, cut into small pieces

1 large egg plus 1 large egg yolk, beaten

This is a take on frangipane, the classic French custard-and-fruit tart, that replaces the more traditional almonds with pine nuts. Plums, nectarines, or other freestone fruits are also wonderful alternatives. It's a delightful tart with tea or coffee in the morning, or after dinner with a sleek sliver of room-temperature triple-cream cow's-milk Explorateur or Brillat-Savarin.

TO MAKE THE TART DOUGH BY HAND: In a bowl, whisk together the flour, sugar, salt, and lemon zest. Add the butter pieces and toss to coat. Using your hands, work quickly to cut in the butter, rubbing it into the flour mixture with your fingertips until the mixture resembles coarse crumbs, with large pieces of butter still visible. Add the whole egg and egg yolk and stir just to combine. Take care not to work the dough too much, or the crust will be tough.

TO MAKE THE TART DOUGH IN A FOOD PROCESSOR: In the work bowl of a food processor fitted with the blade attachment, combine the flour, sugar, salt, and lemon zest and pulse to mix. Add the butter pieces and pulse just until a crumbly mixture with butter pieces the size of small peas forms. Add the whole egg and egg yolk and pulse until the dough just comes together, taking care not to overwork.

Turn the dough out onto a well-floured work surface and gently form a ball. Wrap in plastic wrap and refrigerate for at least 1 hour, or up to 24 hours.

Preheat the oven to 350°F/180°C.

Unwrap the dough and roll out on a lightly floured work surface into a rough rectangle about ⅛ in/3 mm thick. (If the dough is too stiff to roll out, let stand for a few minutes to loosen up.) Cut the dough into six equal pieces and gently press each piece into a 5-in/12-cm tart mold with a removable bottom, pressing it into the corners and trimming any excess. If the dough tears here and there, no worries; simply press the dough into the mold evenly using the tips of your fingers.

Arrange the tart shells on a baking sheet, prick the bottoms all over with a fork, and refrigerate for 10 minutes, then line with parchment paper and fill with dried beans or pie weights. Bake for 10 to 15 minutes, or until the edges are firm. Remove the paper and beans and bake for 3 to 5 minutes longer, or until the bottoms of the shells are firm and dry but not browned. Remove from the oven and let cool completely before filling. Leave the oven on.

TO MAKE THE FILLING: In a bowl, using an electric mixer set on high speed, beat the butter and sugar together until light and fluffy. Beat in the eggs one at a time, followed by the flour, pine nuts, and vanilla. Beat until just combined.

Spoon the filling into the cooled tart shells, dividing it evenly and smoothing the tops with the back of the spoon. Halve the peaches and remove the stones. Cut each half into thin slices and arrange, overlapping, into concentric circles atop the filling of each tart. Bake for 40 minutes, or until the filling in the middle of the tart is fully cooked. It should feel firm to the touch and spring back when lightly pressed. Transfer to a wire rack and let cool for 20 minutes, then remove the tarts from the molds.

Place the tarts on individual plates and place a slice of the cheese alongside. Serve at room temperature.

FOR THE FILLING:

½ cup/115 g unsalted butter, at room temperature

½ cup/100 g sugar

2 large eggs

½ cup/65 g all-purpose flour

½ cup/55 g pine nuts, finely chopped (if chopping in a mini food processor or spice grinder, take care not to grind into a butter)

1 tsp vanilla extract

4 large ripe peaches

6 oz/170 g Explorateur or other soft-ripened triple-cream cheese, cut into 6 equal pieces

BAKED PRUNE PLUMS WITH RED WINE, HONEY, AND ROBIOLA TRE LATTI

SERVES 4

2 tbsp unsalted butter, at room temperature

4 ripe prune plums or other freestone plum variety

2 tbsp wildflower honey

¼ cup/60 ml dry red wine

Freshly cracked black pepper

6 oz/170 g Robiola Tre Latti or other fresh robiola cheese

This is a great late-summer dessert to serve after a family meal. Prune plums are baked with wildflower honey, red wine, butter, and fresh black pepper to create a stunning pan syrup for drizzling over both the plums and the accompanying cheese.

Creamy, tangy, extra-rich Robiola Tre Latti from Piedmonte, Italy, is a fantastic blend of—you guessed it—three kinds of milk: sheep, cow, and goat. When young, the cheese has an incredible cakelike structure that makes it the perfect dessert cheese.

Preheat the oven to 400°F/200°C. Line a baking sheet with parchment paper. Grease the paper with 1 tbsp of the butter.

Halve the plums and remove the stones. Place the plum halves, cut-side down, on the buttered paper. Rub the remaining 1 tbsp butter over the skins. Drizzle the honey over the plums, then drizzle the wine over, and grind some fresh pepper over the top.

Bake for 12 to 15 minutes, or until the plums are just beginning to collapse and the juices in the pan have reduced to a nice, thick syrup. Remove from the oven and let cool to room temperature.

Arrange two plum halves on each of four dessert plates, cut-side down. Slice the cheese into four equal pieces and rest one piece on each plate, against the plums. Scrape the pan syrup from the baking sheet into a small bowl, then drizzle all over the plums and cheese. Serve immediately.

CUCUMBER TEA SANDWICHES WITH FROMAGE BLANC

MAKES 8 TEA SANDWICHES; SERVES 4

1 seedless hothouse (English) cucumber, peeled and cut into slices about ⅛ in/ 3 mm thick

2 tbsp fresh lemon juice

Sea salt and freshly cracked black pepper

4 slices rustic whole-grain bread, crusts removed

4 tbsp/60 ml fromage blanc

1 tbsp minced fresh chives

Many years ago, in London, I discovered a snack I loved: crisp, bright, lemon-soaked cucumber slices on hearty whole-grain bread spread with fresh fromage blanc. It turned a coffee fiend like me into a lover of good English tea instantly. These zesty little sandwiches can also be made with fresh goat cheese or good-quality cream cheese.

Put the cucumber slices in a bowl and toss with the lemon juice, a pinch of salt, and a few grindings of pepper. Cover and let marinate in the refrigerator for 30 minutes.

Lay the bread slices out on a work surface and spread 2 tbsp of the fromage blanc on each of two of the slices, spreading it all the way to the edges. Sprinkle the minced chives over the cheese, then arrange the marinated cucumber slices evenly over the chives. Top the sandwiches with the other two slices of bread. Cut each sandwich into four squares or triangles and serve immediately.

This bright and glorious dish can be piled on a large family-style platter or served as a side on individual plates in a more formal setting. If both yellow and green haricots verts are available, try using half of each for a greater blast of color.

Leonora is a lemony, cakelike goat's-milk cheese from Spain. If you can't find it, this recipe is fantastic with any crumbly fresh goat cheese, such as Caña de Cabra, Bûcheron, or Humboldt Fog. As for the *capocollo*, try it here if available, but if not, there are so many amazing artisanal *salume* makers popping up around the world, I encourage you to seek out alternative products.

Bring a pot of water to a boil over high heat and add a small handful of salt. Have ready a large bowl of water and ice. Add the haricots verts to the boiling water and cook for 5 to 6 minutes, or until tender but still crisp to the bite. Drain in a colander and plunge into the ice water to stop the cooking. As soon as the beans are cool, drain and pat dry with a clean kitchen towel. Set aside.

In a bowl, combine the tomato, basil, parsley, garlic, and olive oil and toss to mix. Season with salt and pepper. Cover and let stand at room temperature for 1 hour, or refrigerate for up to 3 hours (the longer the tomatoes sit, the more pronounced the raw garlic flavor will be); bring to room temperature before serving.

To plate the dish, lay the slices of *capocollo* around the edges of a large platter. Pile the haricots verts in the center and then pour the tomato mixture over the beans. Divide the cheese into eight to twelve equal pieces and distribute evenly around the beans. Serve with plenty of crusty Italian bread.

HARICOTS VERTS WITH LEONORA GOAT CHEESE, CAPOCOLLO SALAMI, AND TOMATOES

SERVES 4 TO 6

Sea salt

1 lb/455 g haricots verts, trimmed

1 ripe large heirloom tomato, cored and cut into small dice

1 tbsp chopped fresh basil

1 tbsp chopped fresh flat-leaf (Italian) parsley

2 garlic cloves, chopped

3 tbsp extra-virgin olive oil

Freshly cracked black pepper

1 lb/455 g *capocollo* salami (also called *coppa*), thinly sliced

8 oz/225 g Leonora or other soft goat cheese

Crusty Italian bread for serving

SAVORY CAKE WITH OVEN-DRIED TOMATOES AND FETA

MAKES ONE 4½-BY-10-IN/11-BY-25-CM
LOAF CAKE; SERVES 4 TO 6

FOR THE OVEN-DRIED TOMATOES:

4 large, ripe but firm plum (Roma) tomatoes,
quartered and seeded

1 tbsp extra-virgin olive oil

1 tsp chopped fresh thyme

1 tsp chopped fresh rosemary

1 tsp sugar

Sea salt and freshly cracked black pepper

This is a phenomenal savory cake for picnics or brunches, served with a crisp salad of garden greens dressed with fresh citrus juices. The base of the cake can be used as a departure for your own whimsy—mix and match whatever clever ingredients you may find lingering around.

The oven-dried tomatoes used in this recipe will keep for a couple of weeks in the refrigerator and are delicious in pastas and eggs or as an antipasto with cheese and *salume*. I recommend doubling the recipe and reserving the extra, as they are really worth having around. Store in tightly sealed jars with sliced garlic and extra-virgin olive oil to cover. As an added bonus, the sweet and fragrant oil from the tomatoes can be drizzled over grilled fish, used in salads, or simply eaten with good crusty bread. On the other end of the spectrum, if you don't have time, substitute good-quality sun-dried tomatoes packed in olive oil.

TO PREPARE THE TOMATOES: Preheat the oven to 200°F/95°C. Line a baking sheet with parchment paper.

In a bowl, combine the tomatoes, olive oil, thyme, rosemary, sugar, a good pinch of salt, and a few grindings of pepper and toss to mix and coat well. Spread the tomatoes, cut-side up, on the prepared baking sheet in a single layer. Bake until the tomatoes are as dry as a juicy raisin, 3 to 4 hours. Let cool completely and set aside. (The tomatoes can be made ahead and refrigerated, tightly covered, for up to 2 weeks.)

Raise the oven temperature to 350°F/180°C. Line a 4½-by-10-in/11-by-25-cm loaf pan with parchment paper.

cont'd

2 cups/255 g all-purpose flour

1 tbsp baking powder

1 tsp sea salt

Freshly cracked black pepper

3 large eggs

½ cup/120 ml extra-virgin olive oil

½ cup/120 ml whole milk

2 oz/55 g Parmigiano-Reggiano cheese, grated

5 oz/140 g feta cheese, cut into ½-in/12-mm cubes

2 tbsp thinly sliced fresh basil

In a medium bowl, whisk together the flour, baking powder, salt, and a few grindings of pepper. In a separate bowl, beat together the eggs, olive oil, and milk until well combined. Slowly whisk the egg mixture into the flour mixture. Switch to a wooden spoon and stir until a thick, smooth batter forms. Add the Parmigiano, feta, oven-dried tomatoes, and basil all at once and stir until the ingredients are just combined.

Pour the batter into the prepared pan and bake for 45 to 50 minutes, or until a wooden skewer inserted into the middle of the cake comes out clean. Transfer to a wire rack and let cool for 10 minutes, then turn the cake out onto the rack and let cool completely. Cut into thick slices and serve. The cake can be wrapped in plastic wrap and refrigerated for up to 4 days.

On my first trip to Bologna over twenty years ago, I visited the culinary landmark and gastronomic treasure known as A. F. Tamburini. To describe this food shrine as a deli would be like calling the Vatican simply the home of a priest. Cheeses, *salume,* fresh pastas, and prepared foods are on display in a riot of Baroque elegance among the marble floors and glistening glass cases.

It was here, while staring at the golden chickens spinning on the majestic copper spit roaster, that a perfume of remarkable glory and elegance caught my attention. In the small kitchen behind me, the oven doors were opening to reveal a massive cast-iron roasting pan holding a bubbling sea of roasted cherry tomatoes. Bright red here, blackened burned spots there, it was a vision of purity and simplicity that I have carried with me ever since.

These tomatoes can stand alone as a dramatic centerpiece to accompany roasted chicken or grilled fish; serve them hot from the oven and straight from the pan, placing it in the center of the table. But when cooled to room temperature, a few spoonfuls atop creamy, rich Burrata are transcendent. If the tomatoes are naturally super-sweet, the amount of sugar can be reduced.

Position a rack in the upper third of the oven and preheat to 500°F/260°C.

In a large bowl, toss the tomatoes with the olive oil, 2 tsp salt, the sugar, chile, and a few grindings of black pepper. Add the oregano and toss once or twice more to distribute.

Transfer the tomatoes into a ceramic baking dish, making sure to scrape all of the seasoned oil from the bottom of the bowl over the tomatoes. Place on the upper rack of the oven and roast for 12 to 15 minutes, or until the tomatoes begin to collapse and turn deep golden brown, with a few black burnt spots on top. Remove from the oven and let cool to room temperature.

To serve, simply cut the balls of Burrata in half and arrange on a serving dish or individual plates. Divide the roasted tomatoes among the Burrata halves and drizzle with the roasting juices and oil from the baking dish.

OVEN-ROASTED CHERRY TOMATOES WITH FRESH OREGANO AND CHILES ON BURRATA

SERVES 8

2 lb/910 g cherry tomatoes, stemmed

¼ cup/60 ml extra-virgin olive oil

Flaky sea salt

2 tsp sugar

1 small fresh or dried red chile, thinly sliced crosswise, or ½ tsp red pepper flakes

Freshly cracked black pepper

Leaves from 2 fresh oregano sprigs, or 1 tsp dried oregano

Four 8-oz/225-g balls fresh Burrata cheese

FRIED NEAPOLITAN SKEWERS WITH CHERRY TOMATOES AND FRESH MOZZARELLA (SPIEDINI)

MAKES 12 SKEWERS; SERVES 6

12 balls bocconcini or ciliegine mozzarella, halved

2 tbsp thinly sliced fresh basil

Freshly cracked black pepper

About ½ lb/115 g good-quality rustic bread, crust removed, cut into twenty-four 1-in/2.5-cm cubes

12 small cherry or Sweet 100 tomatoes, halved

2 large eggs, beaten

½ cup/65 g all-purpose flour

½ cup/55 g dried bread crumbs

¾ cup/180 ml olive oil

Sea salt

A lovely way to start a hot summer evening, these fanciful skewers of fried fresh mozzarella, sweet cherry tomatoes, and good-quality bread with a dense crumb are kind of a Neapolitan take on the famous Italian grilled cheese sandwiches called *mozzarella in carrozza*.

To gild this lily even further, chop up a few good-quality anchovies into a paste with a drop or two of extra-virgin olive oil and spread onto the slices of bread before assembling the skewers.

The *spiedini* are best served immediately after they have cooled down enough to eat, so it is a good idea to get everything ready ahead of time and let everyone stand around in anticipation!

In a bowl, combine the mozzarella, basil, and a few grindings of pepper. Set aside.

Assemble the *spiedini* onto wooden skewers. For each skewer, start with a bread cube, a piece of mozzarella, a cherry tomato half, another piece of bread, another mozzarella piece, and finally the other half of the tomato on top. Continue until all 12 skewers are assembled.

Beat the eggs in a shallow bowl. Put the flour on a small plate, and pour the bread crumbs on another small plate.

Heat the olive oil in a large sauté pan or skillet over medium heat until hot but not smoking. (A piece of bread should begin to sizzle immediately when placed in the oil.)

Dredge the skewers in the flour, then in the beaten eggs, and finally in the bread crumbs, turning to coat evenly.

Fry a few skewers at a time, about 30 seconds on the first side, then turn over and fry the opposite side for another 30 seconds. Turn again twice, frying the other two sides for about 15 seconds each. The skewers should be deep golden brown and crispy all around. Transfer to paper towels to drain and sprinkle with a little salt while still warm. Repeat to cook the remaining skewers.

Serve hot (but not piping hot, to avoid burning mouths on the melted cheese and tomato juices)!

Long ago, I worked with a Sicilian cook who invited me over to his house for dinner after a long night behind the stove. Unfortunately, he forgot to tell his wife. In classic form, after receiving a quick admonishing in their delightful dialect, he appeared with a loaf of crusty bread, a bowl of roasted peppers, fresh mint and garlic, a glass of last night's wine, and a chunk of humble pecorino. This was not the meal, but merely meant to stall for time while water could be brought to a boil for spaghetti.

The pasta that followed was delicious, but it was these brilliant peppers that have stayed in my imagination over the years.

Caña de Oveja is a creamy, tangy, almost fluffy sheep's-milk cheese made in Murcia, in southeastern Spain. Very similar in appearance to the French goat's-milk cheese Bûcheron, it is one of my all-time favorites. A tart and creamy ripened goat cheese would be a wonderful substitute if Caña de Oveja is not available.

Arrange the bell peppers over the open flame of a gas stovetop burner or grill, or under the broiler. Roast for about 10 minutes, turning occasionally with tongs to evenly blacken the bell peppers on the outside, until there's a slight give when squeezed.

Let the roasted bell peppers cool for 10 minutes. Rinse under cold water, pushing off the burnt skins with your fingers. Discard the skins. Open the bell peppers with your fingertips and discard the seeds, ribs, and stems.

Cut the bell peppers lengthwise into strips about ½ in/12 mm wide and put them in a small bowl. Add the olive oil, mint, and garlic and toss to mix. Transfer the dressed peppers to a ceramic or glass jar with a tight-fitting lid and close the jar tightly. Let the peppers stand for at least 1 hour at room temperature, or preferably overnight. (The peppers will keep, tightly covered in the refrigerator, for up to 1 week.)

Lay the peppers out on a serving platter and crumble the cheese over the top. Serve cold or at room temperature.

ROASTED PEPPERS WITH FRESH MINT, GARLIC, AND CAÑA DE OVEJA

SERVES 6 TO 8

4 or 5 large bell peppers, preferably a mix of red, orange, and yellow

3 tbsp extra-virgin olive oil

¼ cup/7 g fresh mint leaves, roughly torn or chopped

2 garlic cloves, thinly sliced

8 oz/225 g Caña de Oveja or other soft-ripened sheep's-milk or goat cheese

CALZONE WITH SEARED PEPPERS, FRESH SAGE, AND RICOTTA

SERVES 4

FOR THE DOUGH:

¾ cup/180 ml lukewarm water

1¼ tsp active dry yeast

¼ tsp sea salt

¼ tsp sugar

1¾ cups/225 g all-purpose flour

3 tbsp extra-virgin olive oil

While handmade pizzas have taken both the professional and home kitchen by storm over the past few years, the calzone is not to be overlooked. Simply a folded-over pizza, the variations on fillings are just as endless.

Dulcetta peppers are small, sweet, brightly colored peppers that are fantastic simply sautéed over a high heat in a little extra-virgin olive oil. They can be cut in halves or quarters for this recipe, and should still retain their inner crunch after being cooked.

TO MAKE THE DOUGH: Pour the warm water into a large bowl. Sprinkle the yeast on the surface of the water, along with the salt and sugar. Let stand for 5 minutes, or until the yeast is dissolved and creamy, and then add 1 cup/130 g of the flour. Stir until all the flour is incorporated and a very wet and sticky starter dough forms. Place a kitchen towel over the bowl and let stand at room temperature until doubled in bulk, about 2 hours.

Uncover the bowl and add the remaining ¾ cup/95 g flour and 2 tbsp of the olive oil. Using a wooden spoon, stir until most of the flour is incorporated, then turn the dough out onto a generously floured work surface and knead until the dough is still slightly sticky but elastic, with a nice spring when you touch it, 5 to 10 minutes. Pat the dough into a ball, return it to the bowl, rub with the remaining 1 tbsp olive oil, cover, and let rest until it doubles in size, about 1 hour longer.

Heat 2 tbsp of the olive oil in a large sauté pan or skillet over medium-high heat until hot but not smoking. Add the Dulcetta peppers and sage leaves. Sauté for 5 or 6 minutes, or until the peppers begin to soften and are nicely colored. Remove from the heat and let cool to room temperature.

Preheat the oven to 500°F/260°C.

Mix the ricotta and Pecorino in a medium bowl until just combined. Set aside.

Divide the dough into four equal pieces. On a well-floured work surface, flatten and stretch each piece of dough with your fingertips to form a circle roughly 6 in/15 cm in diameter. Divide the cheese mixture evenly among the centers of the dough disks. Divide the roasted peppers evenly atop the cheese. Tear the anchovy fillets (if using) into large pieces and scatter over the peppers. Season with plenty of freshly cracked pepper.

Fold the dough rounds over gently to create a half-moon shape and pinch the edges together to seal well. Place the calzone on a baking sheet lined with parchment paper and brush with the remaining 4 tbsp/60 ml olive oil.

Bake for 15 to 20 minutes, or until the calzone are deep golden brown on top and crisp on the bottom. Some of the cheese may leak out and fry on the pan and, if not too burnt, by all means scrape these tasty bits up with a metal spatula and serve atop the hot calzone!

6 tbsp/90 ml extra-virgin olive oil

6 oz/170 g Dulcetta peppers or other small sweet peppers, preferably a mix of orange and red, seeded and thinly sliced

8 large fresh sage leaves, roughly torn

8 oz/225 g fresh ricotta cheese

2 oz/55 g Pecorino Romano cheese, grated

4 good-quality anchovy fillets (optional)

Freshly cracked black pepper

FRIED EGGPLANT WITH RICOTTA SALATA, BASIL, AND MINT

SERVES 4 TO 6 AS A SIDE DISH

About ½ cup/120 ml extra-virgin olive oil

2 firm globe eggplants, cut into slices about ¼ in/6 mm thick

4 oz/115 g ricotta salata cheese, thinly sliced

6 to 8 large fresh basil leaves, whole or roughly chopped

6 fresh mint leaves, whole or roughly chopped

Freshly cracked black pepper

This dish actually originates from the toppings to my wife's favorite pasta, *pasta alla Norma,* which is macaroni dressed with a simple tomato sauce and topped with slices of fried eggplant, ricotta salata, loads of fresh basil, and plenty of fruity Sicilian extra-virgin olive oil. Named after the opera *Norma* by Sicilian composer Vincenzo Bellini, *pasta alla Norma* in many ways epitomizes Sicilian cooking: simple, fresh ingredients treated with respect and passion.

There is a delightful reference to the dish in *The Snack Thief,* one of Andrea Camilleri's crime novels (a guilty pleasure of mine). The series follows the exploits of Sicilian Detective Inspector Montalbano, who has a love of good food:

> "Why don't you stay and eat with me?"
> Montalbano felt his stomach blanch. Signora Clementina was sweet and nice, but she probably lived on semolina and boiled potatoes. "Actually, I have so much to do . . ."
> "Pina, the housekeeper, is an excellent cook, believe me. She's made *pasta alla Norma*—you know, the one with fried eggplant and ricotta salata."
> "Jesus!" said Montalbano, sitting back down.

Serve this version as an antipasto along with roasted peppers and some good-quality tuna preserved in oil, or as a vegetable side, or *contorno,* to just about any main course.

Heat a large skillet or griddle over medium heat. Add 1 tbsp of the olive oil, swirl to coat the pan bottom, and add a few of the eggplant slices. Drizzle a bit more of the olive oil over the slices and fry for 5 to 7 minutes, or until deep golden on the bottom. Turn the slices and fry until deep golden on the second side and cooked through, 3 to 4 minutes longer. Transfer to a serving dish. Repeat to cook the remaining eggplant, using most of the olive oil. Lay the slices overlapping slightly on the plate as they are finished.

Crumble the cheese over the cooked eggplant. Scatter on the fresh basil and mint. Season with plenty of freshly cracked pepper and drizzle one more splash of olive oil over the whole dish. Serve warm or at room temperature.

Eggplant Parmigiana is a typical southern Italian dish loved the world over. Contrary to the name, the dish does not originate in Parma, but is, rather, a nod to the Parmigiano-Reggiano used to bread slices of eggplant before they are fried in olive oil and baked with tomato sauce.

Eggplant is one of those vegetables, like mushrooms, that takes as much oil as you give it, which can result in a very heavy, greasy dish no matter how high the quality of olive oil used. Baking the slices of breaded eggplant, however, requires much less oil, and results in a crispy breading that keeps this dish lighter than usual.

In this slight variation on the classic, the eggplant slices are filled with provolone cheese before getting breaded. The cheese not only melts inside, but oozes out during baking and fries on the pan, creating crisp laces of cheese that are impossible to not break off and devour while cooking.

PROVOLONE-STUFFED EGGPLANT PARMIGIANA

SERVES 8

FOR THE EGGPLANT STACKS:

2 firm globe eggplants, of the same size and shape

About 1 lb/455 g provolone cheese, thinly sliced

2 tbsp extra-virgin olive oil, plus ½ cup/120 ml

6 oz/170 g Parmigiano-Reggiano cheese, grated

1½ cups/170 g dried bread crumbs

¼ cup/10 g roughly chopped fresh flat-leaf (Italian) parsley

4 large eggs

TO PREPARE THE EGGPLANT STACKS: Trim the green stems off the eggplants and cut into rounds about ⅜ in/1 cm thick. You should be able to get 16 slices from each eggplant.

Stack the eggplant slices in same-size pairs. Slip a slice of provolone between the two slices of eggplant in each stack. Tear the cheese slices in half to fit the smaller rounds of eggplant. It is okay if some of the cheese is sticking out. Reserve the remaining provolone.

Preheat the oven to 425°F/220°C. Line two baking sheets with parchment paper and grease the paper on each with 1 tbsp of the olive oil.

In a large, shallow bowl, combine the 6 oz/170 g Parmigiano, bread crumbs, and parsley and stir to mix well. In a separate shallow bowl, beat the eggs until well blended.

Dip an eggplant stack into the beaten egg, shaking off any excess. Press into the crumb mixture, turning to coat well on all sides, then shake off the excess. Place on a prepared baking sheet. Continue until all of the eggplant stacks are breaded, arranging them on the baking sheets so that they are not too close together.

Drizzle the ½ cup/120 ml olive oil over the top of the eggplant and place in the oven. Bake for about 20 minutes, or until golden and crisp on the bottom. Remove from the oven and turn the stacks carefully with a metal spatula. Return to the oven and bake for 10 minutes longer, or until golden and crisp on the second side. Remove from the oven and let cool completely on the baking sheets.

WHILE THE EGGPLANT IS BAKING, MAKE THE SAUCE: In a large sauté pan, heat the olive oil over medium heat until hot but not smoking. Add the shallot and garlic and stir well. Reduce the heat to low and cook until the shallot is translucent and lightly golden on the edges, and the garlic is aromatic and lightly golden, 2 to 3 minutes.

Add the tomatoes, juices and all. Season with salt and pepper, then add the torn basil to the pan. Raise the heat to medium-high and continue cooking, stirring often, until the sauce has thickened, 10 to 12 minutes. (The key to a great marinara is slightly higher heat for less time, so that the fresh tomato flavor remains intact while the sauce tightens to the right consistency.) Taste and adjust the seasoning. Remove from the heat and let cool to warm, about 10 minutes. Transfer the cooled sauce to a food processor fitted with the blade attachment and process to a smooth purée. You should have about 3 cups/720 ml.

To assemble the dish, spread 1 cup/240 ml of the sauce over the bottom of a 9-by-13-in/ 23-by-33-cm ceramic baking dish. Arrange the baked eggplant stacks on top of the sauce *au cheval,* or slightly overlapping like the shingles on a roof. Pour another 1 cup/240 ml of the sauce in between the slices as you work. Pour the remaining 1 cup/240 ml sauce over the top. Sprinkle with the ¼ cup/30 g Parmigiano. Tear the slices of reserved provolone into large pieces and scatter over the Parmigiano. Drizzle with olive oil and top with the chopped basil.

Bake for 20 minutes, or until the cheese on top is melted and golden and the dish is heated through. Serve immediately.

FOR THE SAUCE:

2 tbsp extra-virgin olive oil

1 large shallot, finely chopped

2 or 3 garlic cloves, slightly smashed

One 28-oz/800-g can plum (Roma) tomatoes, preferably San Marzano, chopped, with juices

Sea salt and freshly cracked black pepper

2 large fresh basil leaves, torn into large pieces

¼ cup/30 g freshly grated Parmigiano-Reggiano cheese

Extra-virgin olive oil for drizzling

3 or 4 large fresh basil leaves, roughly chopped

SEARED AND ROASTED EGGPLANT WITH OREGANO AND MOZZARELLA DI BUFALA

SERVES 4

1 firm globe eggplant, cut lengthwise into quarters with stem and blossom ends attached

1 tbsp chopped fresh oregano

¼ tsp red pepper flakes

3 tbsp extra-virgin olive oil, plus more for drizzling

Sea salt and freshly cracked black pepper

4 oz/115 g fresh mozzarella di bufala, torn into bite-size pieces

Really good-quality fresh and flavorful mozzarella made from water buffalo's milk is a hard thing to find outside of Italy. Still, there are times when a high-caliber mozzarella di bufala, or a mozzarella made with cow's milk, known in Italy as *fior di latte,* can be found, whether it is an imported product or something made locally by expert artisans. Whenever you find such a thing, stop what you're doing and buy it!

This eggplant preparation was created by pizza makers in Italy, and is often served with fresh tomato sauce—a great way to enjoy the flavors of hot and milky mozzarella.

Preheat the oven to 450°F/230°C.

In a large bowl, toss the eggplant quarters with the oregano, red pepper flakes, and 2 tbsp of the olive oil and season with salt and black pepper.

Heat a large sauté pan or skillet over medium-high heat. Add the remaining 1 tbsp olive oil to the pan and swirl to coat the pan bottom. Place the eggplant wedges in the hot pan, cut-sides down. Place another sauté pan on top of the eggplant and then a third pot or something heavy to weigh them down. Sear the eggplant for about 5 minutes. Remove the weights and gently loosen the eggplant from the hot pan with a metal spatula so they don't stick. They should be deep golden brown on the seared side, and almost burnt in spots. Turn the eggplant wedges onto the other cut sides and return the weights. Continue cooking for another 5 minutes, or until both sides are evenly colored.

Transfer the eggplant quarters to a baking sheet, skin-side down. Sprinkle the mozzarella over the eggplant, dividing it evenly. Drizzle with olive oil and bake for 8 to 10 minutes, or until the cheese is just beginning to melt and bubble.

Serve hot, making sure to scrape any of the yummy melted mozzarella left on the pan to divide among the diners.

This bright and delicate soup is perfectly suited for an elegant summer lunch. Although a good homemade chicken or vegetable broth can be used for a deeper flavor, the simple, clean flavors of the zucchini and onions shine through with the use of fresh water. Serve either hot with toasts of wheat bread fried in olive oil, or chilled with a drizzle of fruity extra-virgin olive oil and a few gratings of fresh lemon zest.

In a large saucepan, heat the olive oil over medium heat until hot but nowhere near smoking. Add the onions and reduce the heat to low. Cook the onions, stirring, until translucent and just beginning to turn gold around the edges, 5 to 7 minutes. Add the garlic and cook for 1 minute, or until just golden and aromatic.

Raise the heat to high, add the zucchini and basil, and season with salt and pepper. Stir well and cook for another minute, then add the cold water and bring to a boil. Reduce the heat to low and simmer until the zucchini is tender, about 20 minutes.

Remove from the heat and add the goat cheese and lemon juice, stirring well until the cheese is thoroughly melted. Let cool slightly, then, working in batches, pour the soup into a food processor fitted with a blade attachment and pulse until smooth, taking care not to burn yourself. Return the soup to the saucepan and rewarm gently, if needed.

Taste and adjust the seasoning. Ladle into warmed bowls and serve hot.

ZUCCHINI AND FRESH GOAT-CHEESE SOUP

SERVES 4 TO 6

¼ cup/60 ml extra-virgin olive oil

2 small yellow onions, chopped

1 garlic clove, chopped

4 medium zucchini, trimmed and cut into medium dice

4 large fresh basil leaves, roughly chopped

Sea salt and freshly cracked black pepper

4 cups/960 ml cold water

6 oz/170 g fresh goat cheese, at room temperature

2 tbsp fresh lemon juice

GRILLED FLATBREADS WITH ZUCCHINI AND ROBIOLA BOSINA

MAKES 8 INDIVIDUAL FLATBREADS

FOR THE DOUGH:

¾ cup/180 ml warm water

1½ tsp active dry yeast

3 tbsp extra-virgin olive oil,
plus more for rubbing

2 cups/255 g all-purpose flour

1 tsp sea salt

FOR THE HERB OIL:

½ cup/120 ml extra-virgin olive oil

1 tbsp finely chopped fresh thyme

1 tbsp finely chopped fresh rosemary

Zest of 1 lemon

Freshly cracked black pepper

These grilled flatbreads, using a delicious homemade dough, are wonderfully versatile, and the topping possibilities are endless: tangy Robiola and soppressata salami; Brie and Madrange ham; or grilled vegetables with soft-ripened cheese. They can be prepared ahead of time and wrapped in sheets of parchment, then piled high on a cake stand or wooden board for guests to grab and devour.

Robiola Bosina, also called Robiola Due Latti, is a soft-ripened cheese made of a mix of sheep's and cow's milk from Piedmonte, Italy. It has the texture of Brie, with the clean, tangy flavors of sheep's milk. Any soft-ripened cheese would be welcome on these flatbreads, including Taleggio, Bianca Langa, and Fromager d'Affinois.

TO MAKE THE DOUGH: Pour the warm water into a large bowl. Sprinkle the yeast on the surface of the water. Let stand for 5 minutes, or until the yeast is dissolved and creamy. Add the 3 tbsp olive oil and mix well. Add the flour and salt all at once and stir until a sticky dough forms. Turn the dough out onto a well-floured work surface and knead for about 5 minutes, or until the dough is smooth and elastic. Roll into a ball, return to the bowl, and rub with a little olive oil. Cover with a kitchen towel and let rest in a warm place for at least 1 hour, until doubled in bulk.

MEANWHILE, MAKE THE HERB OIL: In a small bowl, combine the olive oil, thyme, rosemary, lemon zest, and a grinding of pepper. Set aside at room temperature.

Build a hot fire in a charcoal grill and let it burn until the coals are red hot with a coating of ash, or preheat a gas grill to its highest heat.

Cut the zucchini lengthwise into slices about ⅛ in/3 mm thick and drizzle with the 1 tbsp olive oil. Arrange on the grill directly over the heat and cook for 4 to 5 minutes, or until nicely grill-marked. Turn the zucchini and continue grilling until tender yet still slightly crisp, 2 to 3 minutes longer. Transfer to a plate to cool.

Lightly oil a baking sheet. Divide the dough into eight equal pieces. On a well-floured work surface, flatten and stretch each piece of dough with your fingertips to form a rectangle about 6 by 3 in/15 by 7.5 cm. Arrange on the prepared baking sheet, cover with a clean kitchen towel, and let rise for 20 minutes, or until almost doubled in bulk.

When the flatbreads have risen, brush them with some of the herb oil, sprinkle with sea salt, and place, oiled-side down, on the grill. Brush the tops of the flatbreads with more of the herb oil and grill for 3 or 4 minutes, until puffed up and deep golden on the grill side, with a few burn spots here and there and nice grill marks.

Using a pair of kitchen tongs, turn the flatbreads and grill until both sides are well marked and the dough is cooked through, about 2 to 3 minutes longer. Transfer to wire racks to cool slightly.

Slice the cheese into eight pieces and lay one atop each flatbread, then spread loosely down the middle of the warm flatbread. Arrange the ribbons of grilled zucchini atop the cheese, dividing them evenly, and serve hot or at room temperature.

4 small zucchini, trimmed

1 tbsp extra-virgin olive oil

Coarse or flaky sea salt

8 oz/225 g Robiola Bosina or other soft-ripened cheese, at room temperature

PIZZA WITH SQUASH BLOSSOMS, BURRATA, AND ANCHOVIES

MAKES FOUR 10-IN/25-CM
INDIVIDUAL PIZZAS

FOR THE DOUGH:

¾ cup/180 ml warm water

1½ tsp active dry yeast

3 tbsp extra-virgin olive oil,
plus more for rubbing

2 cups/255 g all purpose flour

1 tsp sea salt

16 small zucchini blossoms

Coarse cornmeal or all-purpose flour
for dusting

1 lb/455 g fresh Burrata cheese

I can't think of a single pizza that has more elegance, both in flavor and visual beauty, than this classic Roman staple. It can be found all over the city, most often where *pizza a taglia,* or "cut to order," pizza is offered.

I have found that fresh, locally made Burrata—which is far easier to find for most of us than fresh, locally made mozzarella di bufala—works wonders on a pizza, with its rich milk flavor and creamy melting qualities. If you do get your hands on the ultra-fresh *bufala,* by all means substitute it for the Burrata.

TO MAKE THE DOUGH: Pour the warm water into a large bowl. Sprinkle the yeast over the surface of the water. Let stand for 5 minutes, or until the yeast is dissolved and creamy. Add the olive oil and mix well. Add the flour and salt all at once and stir until a sticky dough forms. Turn the dough out onto a well-floured work surface and knead for about 5 minutes, until the dough is smooth and elastic. Roll into a ball, return to the bowl, and rub with a little olive oil. Cover with a clean kitchen towel and let rest in a warm place until doubled in bulk, about 1 hour.

Divide the dough into four equal pieces and roll them into individual balls on a lightly floured surface. Cover again with the kitchen towel and let rest for 20 minutes, or until almost doubled in bulk again.

If using a pizza stone, place on the lowest rack of the oven, or invert a baking sheet and do the same. Preheat the oven to the highest setting it has, at least 500°F/260°C.

Rinse the zucchini blossoms and discard the pistils and stems. Gently tear open the flowers and pat them dry on a kitchen towel. Set aside.

Working with one pizza at a time, on a well-floured work surface, flatten and stretch a dough piece with your fingertips to form a circle about 10 in/25 cm in diameter. Scatter a small amount of coarse cornmeal or flour onto a pizza peel or rimless baking sheet and transfer the pizza dough round onto it.

cont'd

4 anchovy fillets

4 tbsp/60 ml extra-virgin olive oil

Sea salt and freshly cracked black pepper

Tear the Burrata into small bite-size pieces and scatter one-fourth across the dough round. Lay one-fourth of the zucchini blossoms over the Burrata, then tear one anchovy fillet into small pieces and dot around the top. Drizzle with 1 tbsp of the olive oil and season with salt and pepper.

Working quickly, open the door to the oven and slide the pizza onto the preheated stone or baking sheet. Close the door and bake for 10 to 12 minutes, or until the cheese is melted and bubbling and the pizza is browned and crisp around the edges. Remove the pizza from the oven using the peel or baking sheet and transfer to a cutting board or an individual dinner plate. Continue with the remaining dough and topping ingredients until all of the pizzas are done. Serve each pizza hot out of the oven or warm when they are all completed.

AUTUMN

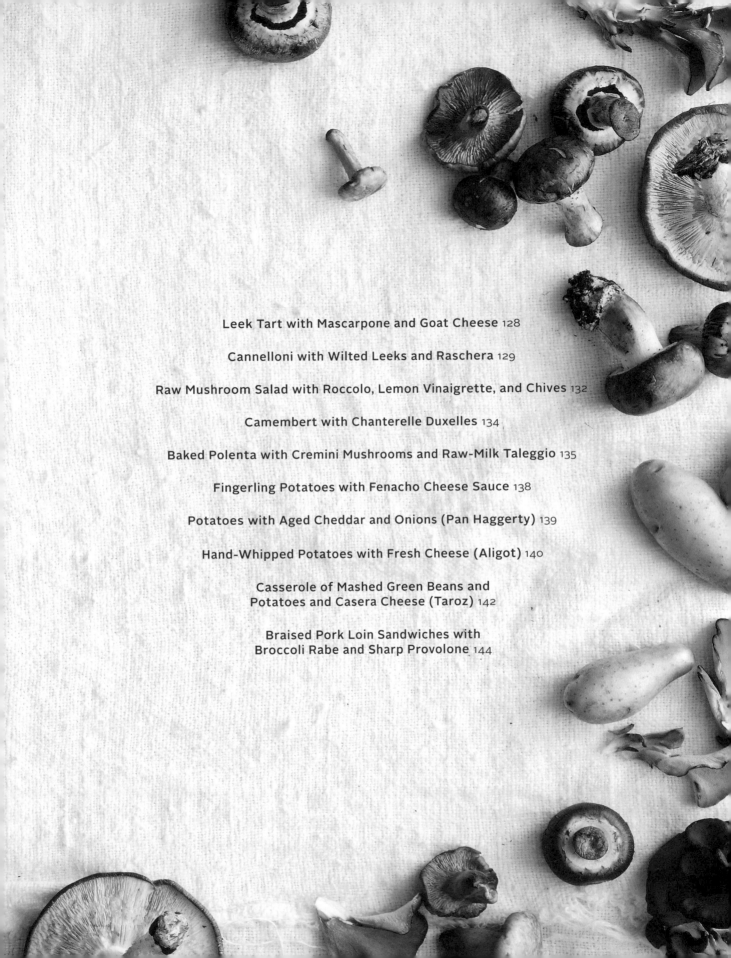

LEMONY QUINCE JAM

MAKES ABOUT 3 CUPS/680 G

2 quince

2¼ cups/540 ml water

Zest and juice of 1 lemon

2 cups/400 g sugar

Quince is a rather mesmerizing fruit to behold; the trees are magnificent, and the yellow fruits so beautiful in their imperfect shape. Quince are strangely inedible raw, yet they develop the most delightful honey and apple flavors when the fruits are cooked.

The root of the word "marmalade" is actually *marmello*, the Portuguese word for quince. There is a long tradition of quince jams throughout not only Portugal and Spain, but also Sicily and England; in all of these places, the jam may be dried after cooking to form a thick paste for cutting or jarred like a more common fruit jam and spooned onto salty or strong cheeses.

This jam is best known for serving on piquant Manchego and similar firm and mild cheeses, but it can be dolloped on grilled meats as well—mix in a little strong mustard powder for an impromptu *mostarda* on pork chops.

Have ready six clean ½-pt/225-g canning jars with new lids and rings.

Wash and dry the quince. Halve the quince. Do not peel. Using the large holes on a box grater-shredder, shred the quince halves, rotating around the core. You should have about 3 cups/420 g packed, shredded quince.

In a large, heavy-bottomed saucepan over high heat, bring the water to a boil. Add the shredded quince and lemon zest and juice. Return to a boil, then reduce the heat to medium-low and simmer until the quince is tender and cooked through, about 10 minutes.

Add the sugar, raise the heat to high, and return to a boil once more, stirring constantly to dissolve the sugar. Reduce the heat to medium-high and cook, stirring occasionally, for 30 to 40 minutes, or until the jam deepens in color to a light orange hue and has thickened enough to coat the back of a chilled metal spoon.

While the jam is cooking, fill a canner fitted with a jar rack or a pot fitted with a steamer rack about halfway full of water and place over high heat. Bring a teakettle of water to a boil at the same time. Meanwhile, wash the jar lids and rings

cont'd

in hot soapy water; rinse thoroughly and put in a bowl of hot water. When the pot of water is hot but not boiling yet, using tongs or a jar lifter, lower the canning jars into the hot water and settle them on the rack. Add more hot water from the teakettle if needed to cover the jars by about 1 in/2.5 cm. Bring the water to a full boil, then adjust the heat for a gentle boil and boil the jars for 10 minutes to sterilize. Using the tongs, transfer to a clean kitchen towel. Reduce the water temperature to a bare simmer.

When the jam is done, using a deep soup-spoon or small ladle, spoon the hot jam into the sterilized jars, preferably while the jars are still hot. Leave a ¼-in/6-mm headspace at the top (but no more than that, or excess air may cause spoilage). Use a damp towel to clean any drips off the rims of the jars. Place the lids on the jars, using the end of a spoon or a chopstick (or a magnet stick, if you have one) to nudge them out of the hot water, and handling them only by the edges. Screw on the rims firmly (but not as tight as possible). Use the tongs to lower the filled jars back into the rack. Raise the heat to achieve a full but gentle boil again, then cover and begin timing; boil for 5 minutes. Remove the jars and let cool completely. Store the jam in a cool, dark place for up to 6 months. Refrigerate after opening.

Halawy dates are a smaller variety than the popular Medjools, with unbelievable honey and brown-sugar flavors and a creamy texture that could easily pass for a soft butter caramel. They are so tender that no chopping is needed, as they will break up in your fingertips to meld harmoniously with the goat cheese.

This cheese-date log is a delightful way to dress up a cheese board for the holidays, or to serve on its own for an afternoon tea with fresh grapes and plain crackers.

With clean hands, mix the goat cheese and the dates together in a bowl until the mixture is a smooth paste. Roll the mixture into a log shape roughly 2 in/5 cm thick and about 8 in/20 cm long and set aside.

Toast the sesame seeds in a small, dry skillet over medium heat for about 1 minute, until just barely turning golden, taking care not to burn them. Remove from the heat and immediately pour the seeds out onto a plate. Let cool completely.

Roll the cheese-date log in the toasted sesame seeds to coat well and serve. The log can be prepared up to 3 hours in advance and refrigerated, but be sure to allow it to come to room temperature before serving.

HALAWY DATE AND GOAT-CHEESE ROLL WITH TOASTED SESAME SEEDS

SERVES 6 TO 8

8 oz/225 g fresh goat cheese

8 oz/225 g Halawy or Medjool dates, pitted

⅓ cup/45 g sesame seeds

FRESH GOAT-CHEESE CUBES WITH FRIED GARLIC CHIPS, ROSEMARY, AND HONEY

MAKES SIX 1-OZ/30-G CUBES; SERVES 6

6 oz/170 g fresh goat cheese

6 small garlic cloves

¼ cup/60 ml extra-virgin olive oil

½ tsp finely chopped fresh rosemary

2 tbsp wildflower honey

Warmed baguette or baguette toasts for serving

These little cubes of fresh goat cheese studded with fried garlic chips are an exciting way to spruce up a cheese board or make a stunning starter. Wait until the last moment before serving to drizzle the honey over the cubes, so the garlic stays crisp.

There is a wonderful scene in *Goodfellas* where Paul Sorvino's character, cooking for his cohorts in prison, develops a clever way of slicing the garlic so thinly with a razor blade that it liquefies in the pan. Spare your fingertips the drama and simply slice the garlic as thinly as you can with a sharp knife for these criminally delicious chips.

Divide the goat cheese into six equal pieces. With clean, dry hands, roll and shape each piece into a small cube. Arrange the goat-cheese cubes on a small plate and set aside.

Slice the garlic cloves lengthwise as thinly as you can. In a small sauté pan or skillet, gently heat the olive oil over low heat until hot but not smoking. Add the garlic slices and cook for about 1 minute, turning them once with a fork, until very lightly golden. Remove the garlic from the oil with the fork and drain on paper towels. (The olive oil can be cooled and saved for another use, such as drizzling over sautéed or grilled vegetables.)

Divide the garlic chips among the tops and sides of the goat cheese cubes, pressing them gently to help them adhere. Sprinkle on the rosemary, then drizzle the honey over the cubes and serve immediately, with fresh or toasted baguette.

PINK LADY APPLE SALAD WITH RADISHES AND SHEEP'S-MILK BLUE CHEESE

SERVES 4

3 crisp, sweet apples such as Pink Lady, washed but not peeled

2 tbsp fresh lemon juice

8 small rainbow or French breakfast radishes, with fresh green tops, if available

4 oz/115 g Bleu de Basques Brebis or other crumbly blue cheese

2 tbsp extra-virgin olive oil

Flaky sea salt

2 tsp wildflower honey

An apple a day? Not a problem—there are so many ways to enjoy the variety of heirloom apples that appear in the farmers' markets every year. They each have their own unique qualities, from crisp and tart to dense and honeyed. At the end of the day, apple taste is a personal thing, and everyone has their favorites. Pink Lady apples are one of mine, a wonderful hybrid of Lady Williams and Golden Delicious that captures the best qualities of both.

This salad is made up of sweet apples, peppery radishes, and buttery rich blue cheese, which is a picnic classic. Bleu des Basques Brebis is an artisanal sheep's-milk blue from the French Pyrenees, and quite a complex-flavored cheese. Bleu d'Auvergne or Roquefort would be good substitutes.

If blue cheese isn't your thing, a semihard sheep's-milk cheese like Abbaye de Belloc from the Benedictine monks of the French Pyrenees, Petit Basque, or any young pecorino would also do nicely here.

Cut the apples in half, then remove the core and seeds with a melon baller or small spoon. Using a sharp knife or a mandoline, cut the apples into slices about ⅛ in/3 mm thick. Put the apple slices in a bowl and toss with the lemon juice to prevent them from browning.

Using the knife or mandoline, cut the radishes into very thin rounds and add to the bowl with the apples. Rinse the radish tops thoroughly, if using, tear into bite-size pieces, and add to the bowl. Crumble the blue cheese into the bowl. Drizzle in the olive oil and a good pinch of salt and gently toss everything together. Throw in some whole radishes if you have some particularly beautiful specimens.

Divide among four plates, drizzle the honey over each salad, and serve.

GREEN APPLE RAVIOLI WITH FRESH GOAT'S-MILK ROBIOLA

SERVES 4 TO 6

FOR THE PASTA DOUGH:

2 cups/255 g all-purpose flour

3 large eggs

1 tsp extra-virgin olive oil

Sea salt

These little pillows of fresh pasta filled with a rich, warm goat cheese mixture perfumed with sweet apples and fried onions make a wonderful first course, followed perhaps by roasted goose or pork loin. (I would even suggest tossing the ravioli with some of the extra juices in the roasting pan.)

The aroma of apples and onions frying together is glorious. The filling for these ravioli may seem less abundant than what you typically find in meat- or ricotta-filled ravioli, but in this case, especially to show off the tender homemade pasta, less is definitely and elegantly more.

I have a collection of wonderful old *raviolatrice,* slender rolling pins with a honeycomb of little cutouts in the wood that form the ravioli. I find them super-easy to use, fun to play with, and helpful in making a lot of ravioli at once (new ones, often called ravioli rolling pins, can be found at many specialty-cookware stores or online). This recipe uses a *raviolatrice* with 1-in/2.5-cm squares. The pasta and filling will work with any ravioli-making method you prefer, of course; but I do recommend keeping them on the bite-size side.

Find a nice tart apple like a Granny Smith for this recipe, as you want to retain that quintessential "apple" flavor throughout the cooking.

TO MAKE THE PASTA DOUGH: Put the flour in a large bowl and make a well in the center. Break the eggs into the center of the well and add the olive oil and a pinch of salt. Using a fork, beat the eggs and oil together. Continue beating, and begin to pull flour from the sides of the well a little at a time. Gradually add more flour from the well to the mix as you work, until all of the flour is incorporated and a sticky dough forms.

Turn the dough out onto a generously floured work surface and knead, adding more flour as needed to prevent sticking, until the dough is soft and supple, about 5 minutes. Roll the dough into a ball and wrap tightly with plastic wrap. Let rest at room temperature for 1 hour.

MEANWHILE, MAKE THE FILLING: In a large sauté pan or skillet, melt the 4 tbsp/55 g butter over medium heat. Peel, core, and finely chop the apples; put them in a bowl; and toss with the lemon juice.

Add the onion to the bowl and toss. Add the apple mixture to the hot butter and cook, stirring occasionally, for 10 minutes, or until the onion is translucent and the mixture is just beginning to turn golden. Remove from the heat and let cool slightly. Transfer the apple mixture to a food processor fitted with the blade attachment. Pulse a few times, just until finely chopped (you do not want the apples and onion puréed).

Transfer the apple mixture to a medium bowl. Crumble in the robiola and toss to distribute, then stir until the filling is well blended. Season with salt and pepper.

To assemble the ravioli, unwrap the dough and cut in half. Return one half to the plastic wrap and keep covered. Cut the other piece of dough in half again. Run one dough piece through a pasta machine with the rollers at the widest setting. Repeat, and then roll the dough twice through each successively narrower setting, until you have a sheet about 22 by 5¾ in/55 by 15 cm. As you work, dust your hands, the rollers, and the dough lightly with flour as needed to prevent sticking, and lay the finished sheet on a lightly floured work surface. Repeat with the second dough piece, then unwrap the second half of the dough and repeat the whole process, for a total of four sheets.

Line a baking sheet with parchment paper. Using the back of a spatula, an offset spatula, or a butter knife, spread half of the filling evenly over one dough sheet, leaving about ⅛ in/3 mm uncovered at the edges. Cover the filling with the second pasta sheet and press gently around the edges to seal. Roll a ravioli pin with 1-in/2.5-cm holes (see recipe introduction) over the filled pasta to press it into little pillow shapes. Separate the ravioli by cutting along the pressed seams with a fluted pastry wheel or the tip of a sharp knife. Arrange the cut ravioli on the prepared baking sheet so they are not touching and cover with a clean kitchen towel.

cont'd

FOR THE FILLING:

4 tbsp/55 g unsalted butter

2 large Granny Smith or other tart green apples

1½ tsp fresh lemon juice

1 small yellow onion, finely chopped

7 oz/200 g goat's-milk Robiola Piemonte or other fresh robiola or goat cheese

Sea salt and freshly cracked black pepper

4 to 6 tbsp/55 to 85 g unsalted butter at room temperature for finishing the pasta

4 oz/115 g Parmigiano-Reggiano cheese, grated

Sea salt and freshly cracked black pepper

Repeat with the remaining two dough sheets and filling. Let the ravioli dry for at least 20 minutes. (The ravioli can be made up to this point ahead of time, and frozen until ready to use. Freeze on the baking sheets for at least 30 minutes, then transfer to zippered bags and freeze for up to 2 weeks.)

When you are ready to cook the ravioli, bring a large pot of water to a boil over high heat and add a small handful of salt. Add the ravioli, stirring gently to prevent sticking, and cook until they float to the surface, about 3 minutes for fresh or 5 to 6 minutes for frozen. (If you are cooking frozen ravioli, cover the pot after you have added the ravioli to the boiling water to help the water return to a boil more quickly, then remove the lid.)

Drain the ravioli in a colander and transfer to a warmed serving bowl. Toss with the room-temperature butter and the Parmigiano. Season with salt and pepper and serve immediately.

Pierre Robert is a decadent soft-ripened, triple-cream cow's-milk cheese from Seine-et-Marne in France. It is essentially the famous Brillat-Savarin cheese, allowed to age in caves a bit longer to develop richer flavors and add a kind of mysteriousness to the texture. The cheese is made in 1.1-lb/500-g wheels, which makes it ideal as a centerpiece for parties. This recipe gilds the lily by topping it with pan-roasted Champagne grapes.

Melt the butter in a large sauté pan or skillet over medium-high heat. Add the grapes, thyme sprigs, and a pinch of salt. Sauté the grapes for 1 or 2 minutes, until golden brown spots appear here and there. Add the sugar and sauté for 30 seconds longer, then raise the heat to high and add the Champagne. Cook for about 1 minute longer, stirring to melt the sugar, until the liquid has reduced and a nice, thick syrup has formed.

Remove from the heat, transfer to a bowl, and let cool slightly. (You can discard the thyme sprigs at this point, though I prefer to leave them in for appearances.) Cover and refrigerate for at least 1 hour, or up to 3 hours.

At least 15 minutes (and up to 30 minutes) before serving, arrange the cheese on a serving platter and bring to room temperature. Spoon the chilled grapes and any juice and syrup remaining in the bowl over the top of the wheel of cheese and serve with the crackers or baguette.

PAN-ROASTED CHAMPAGNE GRAPES WITH PIERRE ROBERT TRIPLE-CREAM CHEESE

SERVES 15 TO 20

1 tbsp unsalted butter

8 oz/225 g fresh champagne grapes or other small, firm table grapes

4 fresh thyme sprigs

Sea salt

1 tbsp sugar

¼ cup/60 ml Champagne or dry white wine

One 1.1-lb/500-g wheel Pierre Robert or Brillat-Savarin cheese

Crackers or sliced baguette for serving

PEAR RISOTTO WITH TESTUN AL BAROLO AND HAZELNUTS

SERVES 4 TO 6

6 cups/1.4 L chicken stock, homemade or good-quality low-sodium purchased

2 ripe Comice or Anjou pears

Juice of ½ lemon

4 tbsp/55 g unsalted butter, plus 3 tbsp at room temperature for finishing the risotto

1 medium shallot, minced

2 cups/400 g Carnaroli or Arborio rice

1 cup/240 ml dry white wine

6 tbsp/45 g freshly grated Parmigiano-Reggiano cheese

Sea salt and freshly cracked black pepper

4 oz/115 g Testun al Barolo cheese, thinly sliced

3 oz/85 g toasted hazelnuts, finely chopped

Testun al Barolo was named by the Slow Food group as the best cheese in Italy in the "drunken" category. It is a semi-hard cheese from Alpine-pasture-raised goats and cows in Piedmonte—which is the same region where Barolo wine is produced. It is fitting that the cheesemakers coat the wheels with Nebbiolo wine grapes and grape must before aging them in wine barrels.

This is a decadent risotto that celebrates the autumn flavors of great wine, ripe pears, and hazelnuts. It can be served as a main course, or to precede a roasted bird or braised beef.

In a saucepan, warm the stock over medium heat. Reduce the heat to medium-low and keep the pan on a burner while you cook the risotto.

Peel, core, and dice the pears, then place them immediately in a small bowl with the lemon juice and toss to coat. Drain the pears and set aside.

Melt the 4 tbsp/55 g butter in a large sauté pan or skillet over medium heat. Add the shallot and cook until translucent, about 5 minutes. Add the rice all at once and stir, being sure to coat all the grains with the butter. Cook for about 5 minutes, stirring constantly, or until the outside layer of the rice grains becomes translucent. Add the wine and stir constantly until completely absorbed, 2 to 3 minutes longer.

Begin adding the hot stock, one ladleful at a time, still stirring constantly. As the stock is absorbed, continue adding more, all the while striking a balance between keeping the rice undulating but not swimming in liquid.

After 15 or 20 minutes, the rice should be cooked, with a nice chew but not crunchy. Stir in the pears and cook for 1 minute to heat them through, then remove from the heat and add the Parmigiano and the 3 tbsp butter, stirring well to create an ultra-creamy risotto. Season with salt and plenty of pepper.

Pour the risotto into a serving bowl or divide among individual bowls. Drape the Testun al Barolo over the top. Sprinkle the hazelnuts on the risotto and serve immediately.

Pumpkins herald the great season of baking in autumn. The moment I see dark orange sugar pumpkins at the farmers' market, I can feel the kitchen calling.

These slender, simple tarts make delightful additions to the autumn dinner table as a side dish. The zing of the goat cheese provides just the right contrast to the rich, savory pumpkin filling, and the aroma of roasted squash mingling with shallots and the perfume of fresh sage is intoxicating. Consider serving as a main course with a big hearty salad.

TO MAKE THE TART DOUGH BY HAND: In a bowl, whisk together the flour and salt. Add the butter pieces and toss to coat. Using your hands, work quickly to cut in the butter, rubbing it into the flour mixture with your fingertips until the mixture resembles coarse crumbs, with large pieces of butter still visible. Add the crème fraîche and stir just to combine. Take care not to work the dough too much, or the crust will be tough.

TO MAKE THE TART DOUGH IN A FOOD PROCESSOR: In the work bowl of a food processor fitted with the blade attachment, combine the flour and salt and pulse to mix. Add the butter pieces and pulse just until a crumbly mixture with butter pieces the size of small peas forms. Add the crème fraîche and pulse until the dough just comes together, taking care not to overwork.

Turn the dough out onto a well-floured work surface and gently form a ball. Slam the dough down on the work surface 10 or 12 times; this will help prevent the crust from rising too much during baking. Wrap the dough in plastic wrap and chill for at least 1 hour, or up to 24 hours.

Preheat the oven to 350°F/180°C.

Unwrap the dough and roll it out on a lightly floured surface to about ⅛ in/3 mm thick. (If the dough is too stiff, let stand for a few minutes to loosen up.) Cut the dough into eight equal pieces and gently press each piece into a 5-in/12-cm tart mold with a removable bottom, pressing it into the corners and trimming away any excess. You may

cont'd

SAVORY PUMPKIN TARTS WITH BÛCHERON

MAKES EIGHT 5-IN/12-CM INDIVIDUAL TARTS

FOR THE TART DOUGH:

2 cups/255 g all-purpose flour

Pinch of sea salt

½ cup/115 g cold unsalted butter, cut into small cubes

⅔ cup/165 ml crème fraîche

FOR THE FILLING:

2 tbsp unsalted butter

One 1-lb/455-g chunk sugar pumpkin, peeled and seeded, flesh cut into medium dice

4 large shallots, thinly sliced

Sea salt and freshly cracked black pepper

4 or 5 fresh sage leaves

½ cup/120 ml water

2 large eggs, beaten

½ cup/120 ml heavy (whipping) cream

4 oz/115 g Bûcheron or other soft-ripened goat cheese

need to re-roll the trimmings to get enough rounds, but try to avoid rolling more than twice. If the dough tears here and there, simply press the dough into the mold evenly using the tips of your fingers.

Arrange the tart shells on a baking sheet, prick the bottoms all over with a fork, and refrigerate for 15 minutes, then line with parchment paper and fill with dried beans or pie weights. Bake for 10 to 15 minutes, or until the edges are firm. Remove the paper and beans and bake for 3 to 5 minutes longer, or until the bottoms of the shells are firm and dry but not browned. Remove from the oven and let cool completely before filling. (If the dough puffs up a little bit, gently flatten with a small spatula.)

TO MAKE THE FILLING: Melt the butter in a large, deep-sided saucepan over medium-high heat. Add the pumpkin and shallots and season with salt and pepper. Add the sage and cook for 5 to 6 minutes, or until the shallots are translucent and the pumpkin takes on a little color.

Add the water and bring to a simmer. Reduce the heat to low, cover, and cook for 15 to 20 minutes, or until the pumpkin is tender.

Remove from the heat and let cool to room temperature. Transfer the cooled pumpkin to a food processor fitted with the blade attachment and process to a smooth purée. Taste and adjust the seasoning. Add the eggs and cream and stir until well blended, then set aside.

Preheat the oven to 425°F/220°C.

Keeping the tart shells on the baking sheet, pour the pumpkin filling into the shells, dividing it evenly. Slice the cheese into eight rounds and place one in the center of each tart. Bake for 45 to 50 minutes, or until the filling is set and the surface is golden brown and the cheese has little browned or even slightly burned spots here and there.

Remove from the oven and let cool for 10 to 15 minutes, then remove the tarts from the molds. Serve warm or at room temperature.

This is the kind of humble greens pie found in farmhouses all over Italy, from Sicily to the Marche and up into Tuscany and farther north, all with their own regional takes. In this version, mineral-rich sautéed Swiss chard and creamy ricotta mingle in a lemon-scented pastry, along with toasted pine nuts and anchovies. Serve for lunch or dinner, either on its own or as a side dish; it goes nicely with chicken or broiled trout or sea bass.

Beet tops, spinach, or a range of other leafy greens can also be used to great success, and the recipe can be augmented with some minced garlic and a handful of chopped olives, salami, or golden raisins.

TO MAKE THE TART DOUGH BY HAND: In a bowl, whisk together the flour, salt, and lemon zest. Add the butter pieces and toss to coat. Using your hands, work quickly to cut in the butter, rubbing it into the flour mixture with your fingertips until the mixture resembles coarse crumbs, with large pieces of butter still visible. Add the crème fraîche and stir just to combine. Take care not to work the dough too much, or the crust will be tough.

TO MAKE THE TART DOUGH IN A FOOD PROCESSOR: In the work bowl of a food processor fitted with the blade attachment, combine the flour, salt, and lemon zest and pulse to mix. Add the butter pieces and pulse just until a crumbly mixture with butter pieces the size of small peas forms. Add the crème fraîche and pulse just until the dough comes together, taking care not to overwork.

Turn the dough out onto a well-floured work surface and gently form a ball. Wrap in plastic wrap and refrigerate for at least 1 hour, or up to 24 hours.

Unwrap the dough and cut in half. Rewrap one half in the plastic and return to the refrigerator. Roll out the other piece of dough on a lightly floured surface to about ⅛ in/3 mm thick. (If the dough is too stiff to roll out, let stand for a few minutes to loosen up.) Fit the dough round into a 10-in/25-cm tart mold with a removable bottom, pressing it into

cont'd

RAINBOW SWISS CHARD AND RICOTTA TART

MAKES ONE 10-IN/25-CM TART; SERVES 6 TO 8

FOR THE TART DOUGH:

2 cups/255 g all-purpose flour

Pinch of sea salt

Zest of 1 lemon

½ cup/115 g cold unsalted butter, cut into small cubes

⅔ cup/165 ml crème fraîche

1¼ lb/570 g rainbow Swiss chard, stems and tough center spines removed

2 tbsp extra-virgin olive oil

Sea salt and freshly cracked black pepper

10 oz/280 g fresh ricotta cheese

3 oz/85 g Pecorino Romano cheese, grated

⅓ cup/45 g pine nuts, toasted

2 anchovy fillets, chopped

1 large egg

1 large egg yolk

the corners, and trim the edges to leave a ½-in/ 12-mm overhang. Prick the bottom all over with a fork and refrigerate for 15 minutes.

MEANWHILE, MAKE THE FILLING: Bring a large pot of salted water to a boil and blanch the chard for 2 or 3 minutes, or until wilted and tender. Remove from the heat and drain in a colander. Let stand until cool enough to handle. Squeeze the chard with your hands to get as much water out as possible, then chop roughly. Squeeze the chopped chard again.

Heat the olive oil in a large sauté pan or skillet over medium-high heat until hot but not smoking. Add the chopped chard and season with salt and pepper. Sauté for 2 or 3 minutes, or until the chard is lightly golden at the edges. Remove from the heat and transfer to a bowl to cool completely.

Add the ricotta, Pecorino, pine nuts, and anchovy fillets to the cooled chard and mix to combine. Taste and adjust the seasoning, then add the whole egg and mix well.

Preheat the oven to 350°F/180°C.

Scrape the filling into the dough-lined tart mold and smooth over evenly. On a lightly floured work surface, roll the second piece of dough out to ⅛ in/3 mm thick. Lay the dough round over the filling and trim the edges to a ½-in/12-mm overhang as well. Roll and pinch the overhanging edges of the two dough pieces to seal all around the tart.

Beat the egg yolk in a small bowl, then brush it over the top of the dough. Using a sharp knife, make several decorative slits in the center of the tart to allow steam to escape.

Place the tart on a baking sheet and bake for 40 to 45 minutes, or until the top is a deep golden brown. Transfer to a wire rack and let cool to room temperature. Remove the tart from the mold, cut into wedges, and serve immediately. Any leftovers can be covered in plastic wrap and refrigerated for up to 3 days.

CORNMEAL WITH FRESH CORN AND CORSU VECCHIU (MAMALIGA)

SERVES 4 TO 6

4½ cups/1 L water

Sea salt

4 ears fresh corn, husks and silks removed

1 cup/140 g coarse cornmeal

3 tbsp unsalted butter, at room temperature

6 oz/170 g Corsu Vecchiu or other semihard sheep's-milk cheese, grated

Freshly cracked black pepper

Mamaliga is the Romanian take on polenta. It's also just fun to say. Often made much thicker than polenta so that it can be sliced and eaten out of hand like bread, its roots as a peasant staple are identical to its Italian cousin's. And like polenta, *mamaliga* has been elevated in modern times to an elegant, creamy cornmeal by adding various seasonal ingredients to it. Here, sweet fresh corn is mixed in to make a porridge that is as hearty as it is flavorful, especially with grilled sausages or roasted game birds.

Corsu Vecchiu is a traditional sheep's-milk cheese from Corsica that has both salty and caramel-like qualities. Its crumbly texture is ideal for topping risotto, pasta, and polenta. A younger pecorino would be a fine substitute.

Pour the water into the top pan of a double boiler directly over medium-high heat, stir in 1 tsp salt, and bring to a boil. Cut the ears of corn in half and add to the water. Reduce the heat to medium-low and simmer until the corn is tender, about 10 minutes. Using tongs, transfer the corn to a plate and set aside. Raise the heat to medium-high and return the water to a rapid boil. Using a wire whisk, stir the boiling water in one direction, creating a vortex. Slowly pour the cornmeal into the vortex in a steady stream, stirring constantly in the same direction. Continue stirring almost constantly even after all the cornmeal is added, for about 5 minutes, or until the cornmeal begins to thicken slightly. Meanwhile, fill the bottom pan of the double boiler with about 2 in/5 cm of water and bring to a boil.

Remove the top pan from the heat and, using kitchen towels or wearing oven mitts, carefully nest the top pan over the boiling water in the bottom pan. Cover, reduce the heat to achieve a gentle simmer, and cook the *mamaliga* for 30 minutes. Uncover, give the cornmeal a good stir with the wire whisk, re-cover, and continue cooking for about 30 minutes longer, or until creamy and cooked through.

Meanwhile, using a serrated knife, cut the corn kernels off the cobs. After the *mamaliga* has been cooking for 1 hour total, add the butter and half of the cheese, stirring to combine well. Add the cooked corn kernels and stir to distribute evenly throughout the cornmeal.

Pour the cornmeal out into a large serving bowl and crumble the remaining cheese over the top. Season with plenty of freshly cracked pepper and serve hot.

LEEKS AND CREAM WITH GRUYÈRE DE COMTÉ

SERVES 4 TO 6

2 lb/910 g small, young leeks

Sea salt

1 tbsp unsalted butter, at room temperature

Freshly cracked black pepper

1 cup/240 ml heavy (whipping) cream

Freshly grated nutmeg

4 oz/115 g Gruyère de Comté, shredded

A slightly decadent take on the leek gratin, tender pieces of poached leeks are draped in heavy cream and Gruyère de Comté. This classic dish makes a great side for pork of almost any cut, or pretty much any roasted or grilled meats.

Young long and slender leeks (no more than 1 in/2.5 cm in diameter) are ideal for this preparation; I can usually find them at farmers' markets. If only larger leeks are available, cut them lengthwise into quarters.

Trim the root ends and dark green tops of the leeks. Discard the tough woody outer leaves. Cut the leeks in half lengthwise, then crosswise into pieces about 3 in/7.5 cm long. Put them in a bowl of cold water. Soak for about 5 minutes, plunging them into the water occasionally to loosen any grit or sand. Rinse and drain the leeks well and pat dry.

Bring a large pot of water to a boil over high heat and add a small handful of salt. Add the leeks, reduce the heat to maintain a gentle simmer, and cook for 7 to 8 minutes, or until the leeks are tender and the tip of a sharp knife pierces them easily. Using tongs, and taking care to keep the pieces as intact as possible, transfer the leeks to a large plate to cool.

Position a rack in the upper third of the oven and preheat to 450°F/230°C.

Grease a 6-by-12-in/15-by-30.5-cm ceramic baking dish with the butter. Arrange the cooked leeks in a single layer in the dish. Season well with salt and pepper.

Heat the cream and a few gratings of fresh nutmeg in a small saucepan over medium-high heat until it begins to bubble all over (not just around the edges). Remove from the heat and pour over the leeks. Scatter the cheese over the top and season again with salt and pepper.

Bake on the upper rack of the oven for 15 to 20 minutes, or until the top of the gratin is a deep golden brown with a few almost-burnt spots here and there. Serve hot.

LEEK TART WITH MASCARPONE AND GOAT CHEESE

SERVES 6 TO 8

1½ lb/680 g small, young leeks

2 tbsp unsalted butter

Sea salt and freshly cracked black pepper

8 oz/225 g mascarpone cheese

8 oz/225 g fresh goat cheese

1 tbsp chopped fresh thyme

One 16½-by-12½ in/42-by-32-cm sheet puff pastry

Gently sweated in a bit of sweet butter until tender, leeks have an aroma that is always mouthwatering. Here they are married with tangy goat cheese and decadent mascarpone in an act of utter simplicity. This tart can be cut into thin slices for two-bite appetizers or big wedges to serve with a crisp salad and a bone-dry white wine.

Position one rack in the middle of the oven and another rack in the lower third. Preheat the oven to 400°F/200°C. Line a baking sheet with parchment paper.

Trim the root ends and dark green tops of the leeks. Discard the tough woody outer leaves. Cut the leeks in half lengthwise. Put them in a bowl of cold water. Soak for about 5 minutes, plunging them into the water occasionally to loosen any grit or sand. Rinse and drain the leeks well and pat dry. Slice them thinly crosswise.

In a large sauté pan or skillet, melt the butter over medium heat. Add the leeks, season with salt and pepper, and cook, stirring often, until just beginning to soften and release some moisture, 3 to 4 minutes. Cover, reduce the heat to low, and continue cooking until the leeks are tender and there is almost no liquid remaining in the pan, 10 to 12 minutes longer. Remove from the heat and let cool.

In a bowl, combine the mascarpone, goat cheese, and thyme. Add about three-fourths of the leeks and mix well.

Place the puff pastry on the prepared baking sheet. Spread the leek mixture evenly over the pastry, leaving a 1-in/2.5-cm border. Roll the edges of the pastry up to the filling on all sides and pinch with your fingers, creating a decorative crust.

Bake on the center rack for 15 minutes. Remove from the oven, scatter the remaining leeks over the top of the tart, and return to the oven, placing it on the lower rack this time. Bake for about 10 minutes longer, until the pastry is cooked all the way through and crisp on the bottom. Serve warm or at room temperature.

Raschera is one of those cheeses that, once you discover it, makes you wonder what you ever did without it. A semi-soft, sweet, mild-but-tangy raw cow's-milk product with a fantastic texture, it only improves with melting. Raschera is a sublime sandwich cheese, or serve it for breakfast with wildflower honey and seedy or grainy toast like a rustic rye.

Made in the mountains around Mondovi near Cuneo in northern Italy, Raschera is sold as young as 1 month old or up to 6 months for spicier, more pronounced flavors. For this recipe, the younger the better.

TO MAKE THE PASTA DOUGH: Put the flour in a large bowl and make a well in the center. Break the whole eggs into the well and add the egg yolk. Using a fork, beat the eggs until well blended. Continue beating, and begin to pull flour from the sides of the well a little at a time. Gradually add more flour from the well to the mix as you work, until all of the flour is incorporated and a sticky dough forms.

Turn the dough out onto a generously floured work surface and knead, adding more flour as needed to prevent sticking, until the dough is soft and supple, about 5 minutes. Roll the dough into a ball and wrap tightly with plastic wrap. Let rest at room temperature for 1 hour.

MEANWHILE, MAKE THE FILLING: Trim the root ends and dark green tops of the leeks. Discard the tough woody outer leaves. Cut the leeks in half length-wise. Put them in a bowl of cold water. Soak for about 5 minutes, plunging them into the water occasionally to loosen any grit or sand. Rinse and drain the leeks well and pat dry.

Melt 10 tbsp/140 g of the butter with the fresh sage leaves in a large sauté pan or skillet over medium heat. Add the leeks and the ½ cup/120 ml water and season with salt and pepper. Stir well, cover, and reduce the heat to maintain a simmer. Cook, stirring occasionally, for about 15 minutes, or until the leeks are tender.

cont'd

CANNELLONI WITH WILTED LEEKS AND RASCHERA

MAKES 16 CANNELLONI; SERVES 6 TO 8

FOR THE PASTA DOUGH:

2 cups/255 g all-purpose flour

2 large eggs plus 1 large egg yolk

FOR THE FILLING:

2½ lb/1.2 kg small, young leeks

12 tbsp/170 g unsalted butter

8 small fresh sage leaves, roughly chopped

½ cup/120 ml water

Sea salt and freshly cracked black pepper

10 oz/280 g Raschera cheese, trimmed of any rind

1½ cups/360 ml heavy (whipping) cream

2 oz/55g Grana Padano or Parmigiano-Reggiano cheese, grated

Tear the Raschera cheese into small pieces and put in a medium bowl. Pour the cream over the cheese and set aside.

Uncover the leeks and raise the heat to high, stirring well until the liquid is evaporated. Add half of the cheese-and-cream mixture and stir well to incorporate into a creamy filling. Remove from the heat and set aside.

Bring a large pot of water to a boil over high heat and add a small handful of salt. While the water is heating, unwrap the dough and cut in half. Return one half to the plastic wrap and keep covered. Cut the other piece of dough in half again. Run one dough piece through a pasta machine with the rollers at the widest setting. Repeat, and then roll the dough twice through each successively narrower setting, until you have a sheet about $\frac{1}{16}$ in/2 mm thick, or even a little thinner. As you work, dust your hands, the rollers, and the dough lightly with flour as needed to prevent sticking, and lay the finished sheet on a lightly floured work surface. Repeat with the second dough piece, then unwrap the second half of the dough and repeat the whole process, for four sheets. Using the tip of a sharp knife, cut the dough sheets into 5-in/12-cm squares.

Have ready a large bowl of water and ice. Cook a few of the pasta squares at a time in the water until al dente, about 1 minute. Using a wire skimmer, plunge the cooked pasta squares into the ice water to stop the cooking, then immediately remove and lay out on a clean work surface. Continue until all the pasta squares are cooked.

Position a rack in the upper third of the oven and preheat to 425°F/220°C. Lightly grease a ceramic baking dish with butter.

Divide the filling evenly among the cooked pasta squares, arranging it in a line down the center of each square. (Do not be surprised when there is not a lot of filling, as this is a great example of stuffed pasta *not* being an excuse to eat the filling!) Fold the squares over to form a filled tube and lay next to each other but not overlapping in the prepared dish. Spoon the remaining Raschera mixture over the filled cannelloni. Sprinkle the Grana Padano over the top and dot with the remaining butter. Place the baking dish in the upper rack of the oven.

Bake on the upper rack of the oven for about 20 minutes, or until the surface is deep golden and bubbly. The edges of the pasta may crisp up and almost burn here and there, which is both characteristic and delicious! Serve hot.

RAW MUSHROOM SALAD WITH ROCCOLO, LEMON VINAIGRETTE, AND CHIVES

SERVES 4

1½ lb/680 g button mushrooms, brushed clean and thinly sliced

½ cup/120 ml extra-virgin olive oil

¼ cup/60 ml fresh lemon juice

Sea salt and freshly cracked black pepper

2 oz/55 g Roccolo or other aged hard cheese

2 tbsp minced fresh chives

Roccolo is a crumbly, creamy cow's-milk cheese from Lombardy in northern Italy, and a cheese well worth seeking out. It is a creation of Arrigoni Valtaleggio, a family-run operation that has played a big role in getting real Taleggio (another of my favorites) to the world outside Italy.

While aging, wheels of Roccolo are washed daily in a bath of salt water and set on pine boards, a technique that helps develop deep, foresty flavors and makes the cheese a match with the earthiness of fresh raw mushrooms. I also love Roccolo's buttermilk-like tang, and find it particularly suited for creamy risottos or hot polenta. Parmigiano-Reggiano, Sovrano, or Grana Padano would be nice substitutes for this recipe.

Put the mushrooms in a large bowl.

In a small jar with a tight-fitting lid, combine the olive oil and lemon juice and season with salt and pepper. Close the jar tightly and shake vigorously until thoroughly blended and a thick, smooth dressing forms.

Pour the vinaigrette over the mushrooms and toss gently to coat without breaking the mushrooms up. Spread the dressed mushrooms on a serving platter in a single layer.

Using a sharp knife, slice the cheese as thinly as you can, then crumble the slices over the dressed mushrooms. Sprinkle the chopped chives over the entire salad and serve immediately.

CAMEMBERT WITH CHANTERELLE DUXELLES

SERVES 6 TO 8

4 tbsp/55 g unsalted butter

1 small shallot, minced

4 oz/115 g chanterelle mushrooms, brushed clean and finely chopped

½ tsp chopped fresh thyme

Sea salt and freshly cracked black pepper

¼ cup/60 ml dry vermouth or white wine

One 8-oz/225-g wheel of Camembert cheese, ripe and at room temperature but not too runny

Baguette or crackers for serving

Duxelles, a finely chopped sauté of mushrooms with shallots, butter, and a little fresh herb, is a classic from the pantheon of great French cuisine. It is very simple to prepare—when chanterelles are in season and low in price, I make a big batch of duxelles, divide it into small baggies, and freeze for use in pastas, beef dishes like Beef Wellington, and spreads for toasts and crusty bread.

This is not only a beautiful presentation for parties, but the combination of the earthy flavors of sautéed mushrooms and the rich and fragrant Camembert is outstanding. While "the real deal" raw-milk Camembert is, sadly, not available in the States, there are some incredible pasteurized versions available; one I love is Le Chatelain from Normandy. A good-quality Brie would also work well with this recipe.

Heat a large sauté pan or skillet over medium-high heat. Add 2 tbsp of the butter and swirl the pan so the butter melts but does not brown. Add the shallot, mushrooms, and thyme. Season well with salt and pepper. Sauté for about 5 minutes, or until the mushrooms are tender and the shallot is translucent. Add the vermouth, raise the heat to high, and cook until the wine has evaporated. Remove from the heat, add the remaining 2 tbsp butter, and stir until the butter is melted. Set aside to cool completely. (The mushroom duxelles can be prepared and kept refrigerated in an airtight container for up to 3 days. Bring to room temperature before serving.)

Using a serrated bread knife, cut the wheel of cheese in half horizontally. Remove the top piece and spread the cooled duxelles evenly over the bottom piece. Place the top of the cheese on the mushroom duxelles and serve with plenty of crusty baguette or crackers. The cheese can be prepared up to 24 hours in advance, and brought to room temperature before serving.

As much as I love the aroma, texture, and—perhaps most of all—romance of polenta that has been cooked in the traditional way with a copper pan, dutifully standing by the stove stirring nonstop for 45 minutes is just not always practical. You may notice, therefore, that I invoke a double-boiler method for polenta, which not only frees the cook from the stove, but actually breaks down the polenta slowly and produces even creamier results. This popular alternative method was taught to me by Carlo Middione, a brilliant chef, culinary anthropologist, and stickler for adherence to the traditional ways, so if it's okay with him, well. . . .

The polenta can be made in advance and finished off in the oven shortly before dinner. Look for the best-quality raw-milk Taleggio you can find, and if cremini mushrooms are unavailable, use whatever variety is in season and fresh.

Pour the water into the top pan of a double boiler directly over medium-high heat, stir in 1 tsp salt, and bring to a boil. Using a wire whisk, stir the boiling water in one direction, creating a vortex. Slowly pour the cornmeal into the vortex in a steady stream (the Italians say *a pioggia:* "like it's raining"), stirring constantly in the same direction. Continue stirring almost constantly even after all the cornmeal is added, for about 5 minutes, or until the polenta begins to thicken slightly. Meanwhile, fill the bottom pan of the double boiler with about 2 in/5 cm of water and bring to a boil.

Remove the top pan from the heat and, using kitchen towels or oven mitts, carefully nest the top pan over the boiling water. Cover, reduce the heat to achieve a gentle simmer, and cook for 30 minutes. Uncover, give the polenta a good stir with the wire whisk, re-cover, and continue cooking for 30 minutes longer, or until creamy and cooked through.

Meanwhile, heat 2 tbsp of the olive oil in a large sauté pan or skillet over medium-high heat until hot but not smoking. Add half of the mushrooms and stir to coat them with the oil, then sear them, turning as needed, until browned on all sides. Resist the urge to stir them in between, so they

cont'd

BAKED POLENTA WITH CREMINI MUSHROOMS AND RAW-MILK TALEGGIO

SERVES 4 TO 6

1 qt/960 ml water

Sea salt

1 cup/140 g coarse cornmeal

6 tbsp/90 ml extra-virgin olive oil

1 lb/455 g cremini mushrooms, brushed clean and cut into slices about ⅛ in/3 mm thick

Freshly cracked black pepper

3 tbsp unsalted butter, at room temperature

½ cup/60 g freshly grated Parmigiano-Reggiano cheese, plus 3 tbsp for sprinkling

6 oz/170 g raw-milk Taleggio cheese, rind removed

4 or 5 fresh sage leaves

get nice and golden brown. Season with salt and pepper. Sauté until tender, a minute or two longer, then scrape onto a plate and set aside. Wipe any burned bits out of the pan, then repeat to cook the remaining mushrooms with another 2 tbsp of the olive oil.

After the polenta has been cooking for 1 hour total, add the butter and the ½ cup/60 g Parmigiano, stirring to combine well. Add all of the mushrooms and stir to distribute evenly throughout the polenta. Pour the polenta out onto a baking sheet and smooth flat to fill the tray evenly. Place in the refrigerator to cool. (The polenta can be made up to this point 1 day ahead of time.)

When the polenta is cool and firm, after about 1 hour, turn it out carefully onto a cutting board and cut into 12 squares. Cut the 12 squares in half on the diagonal to create 24 triangles.

Preheat the oven to 450°F/230°C.

Lightly butter a 6-by-12-in/15-by-30.5-cm ceramic baking dish. Arrange the polenta triangles in the dish, overlapping as needed to fit them snuggly together. Tear the Taleggio into small bite-size pieces and scatter over the polenta. Tear the sage leaves into large pieces and scatter them over the polenta as well. Sprinkle on the 3 tbsp Parmigiano, season with salt, and drizzle the remaining 2 tbsp olive oil over the entire dish.

Bake for 35 to 40 minutes, or until the cheese is melted and golden and the polenta is heated through. Serve immediately.

FINGERLING POTATOES WITH FENACHO CHEESE SAUCE

SERVES 6 TO 8

2 lb/910 g fingerling potatoes, scrubbed but not peeled

1 tbsp sea salt

⅔ cup/165 ml whole milk

8 oz/225 g Fenacho cheese, shredded

Fenacho is a semihard fenugreek-clover-seed-studded goat's-milk cheese from Tumalo Farms in Oregon. The sweet flavor of the fenugreek adds a kind of butterscotch sweetness to the tangy, sharp goat's milk, and is truly a unique table cheese, well worth finding.

Fenacho can lose much of its character when melted directly, but by gently breaking down the cheese in milk over a steady heat, the flavors are preserved and become a decadent sauce for boiled fingerling potatoes.

If Fenacho is unavailable, a semihard goat's-milk Cheddar or Gouda could be substituted, along with 1 tsp fenugreek seeds, lightly toasted.

Put the potatoes in a large pot with cold water to cover by 2 in/5 cm, add the salt, and bring to a boil over high heat. Reduce the heat to medium-low and simmer, partially covered, until the potatoes are tender when pierced with a sharp knife, 25 to 30 minutes. Drain well and transfer to a warmed serving dish.

While the potatoes are cooking, in a heavy-bottomed 2-qt/2-L saucepan over low heat, combine the milk and cheese and cook, stirring occasionally with a whisk or wooden spoon, just until cheese is melted and sauce is smooth (do not let it boil), 8 to 10 minutes.

Remove the cheese sauce from the heat and pour over the potatoes. Serve immediately.

Imagine an English version of the beloved bistro classic Pommes Dauphinoise, wherein onions are added to the potatoes and the mix is covered in sharp Cheddar cheese.

The very best artisan-made Cheddar you can lay your hands on makes all the difference here. Some of my favorites are Montgomery's Cheddar from Neal's Yard Dairy in London; Cabot Clothbound from the East Coast; and Beecher's from the Pacific Northwest. This is one of those times to bring out your well-seasoned cast-iron skillet, which can be brought to the table for serving.

Preheat the oven to 375°F/190°C.

In a large ovenproof skillet or flameproof casserole, melt 8 tbsp/115 g of the butter over medium-low heat. Cook gently until the foam has subsided and the melted butter is translucent but not browned.

Arrange just enough of the sliced potatoes in the melted butter to cover the bottom of the pan. Season with salt and pepper. Scatter on about one-third of the onions and one-third of the cheese and top with about one-third of the remaining potatoes. Repeat the layering of onions, cheese, salt, pepper, and potatoes two more times, ending with a layer of potatoes. Melt the remaining 8 tbsp/115 g butter and drizzle over the top.

Place the pan over medium heat and cook until the bottom layer begins to take on a little color (lift a corner with a spatula to peek). Transfer to the oven and bake for about 30 minutes, or until the potatoes are tender. Raise the oven temperature to 450°F/230°C and cook for another 10 minutes, or until the top is deep golden brown.

Gently loosen the potatoes from the skillet using an inverted spatula. Transfer to a serving plate, cut into wedges, and serve immediately, or serve directly from the hot pan at the table.

POTATOES WITH AGED CHEDDAR AND ONIONS (PAN HAGGERTY)

SERVES 4

1 cup/230 g unsalted butter

2 lb/910 g waxy-skinned potatoes, peeled and thinly sliced

Sea salt and freshly cracked black pepper

3 medium yellow onions, thinly sliced

12 oz/340 g aged Cheddar cheese, shredded

HAND-WHIPPED POTATOES WITH FRESH CHEESE (ALIGOT)

SERVES 6

2 lb/910 g red-skinned, Yukon gold, or other waxy-skinned potatoes

Sea salt

12 oz/340 g Stracchino (also called Crescenza) cheese

1 garlic clove, minced

7 tbsp/100 g unsalted butter, at room temperature

Freshly cracked black pepper

This decadent French take on mash was originally made by monks, using bread instead of potatoes. When spuds arrived from the Americas, they quickly became a peasant staple and found their way into this regional classic from southcentral France.

In France, young fresh tomme is typically used to make *aligot,* but this cheese is harder to find abroad. I have been on a mad mission to replicate the dish with a suitable substitute outside of France. Many cooks use Gruyère, which can produce a rather gluey result, and others use a mixture of Gruyère for the flavor and fresh mozzarella for the texture. The cheese I found that works the best for both the fresh tangy flavor and light airy texture is Stracchino. While the imported Italian originals are glorious, there is an incredible version from Bellwether Farms in Sonoma, California, which they call by Stracchino's other name, Crescenza.

Once the cheese is added, the secret to *aligot* is in the stirring. The motion has to continue in the same direction, and is similar to folding egg whites, using a twist of the wrist. This builds the structure, creating taffy-like ribbons of cheese and potatoes. It's a bit of work, and must be done right before serving, but I can assure you it will all be worth it, especially served with a perfectly cooked hanger steak or grilled sausages and plenty of red wine.

A more rustic version of this dish comes from the Cantal area, where it is known as *truffade.* Rather than mashed, the potatoes are boiled, then sliced and fried in bacon fat or lard. The cheese is added and stirred until melted, and a slice of black truffle is sometimes added. The results should be fairly obvious!

Peel the potatoes and put them in a large pot with cold water to cover by 2 in/5 cm. Bring to a boil over high heat, add a small handful of salt, then reduce the heat to medium and simmer, partially covered, until the potatoes are very tender when pierced with a sharp knife, 20 to 25 minutes.

Meanwhile, slice the cheese into large chunks and set aside.

When the potatoes are cooked, drain well in a colander and pass through a food mill or potato ricer back into the warm pot.

Add the garlic, butter, and a pinch of salt. Using a wooden spatula, stir the potatoes in one direction until a creamy mash forms. Return the pot to the stove over low heat, still stirring constantly, and add the cheese. Continue to stir vigorously in one direction, until the cheese is fully incorporated and melted. The fibers of the cheese should remain intact and result in the desired veil-like, stringy texture.

When the *aligot* is flowing like ribbons, it is ready. Season with more salt and pepper, and pour into a warmed serving bowl. Serve immediately.

CASSEROLE OF MASHED GREEN BEANS AND POTATOES AND CASERA CHEESE (TAROZ)

SERVES 4

Sea salt

1⅓ lb/600 g russet potatoes,
peeled and cut into big chunks

2 oz/55 g pancetta, chopped

1 medium yellow onion, thinly sliced

4 tbsp/55 g unsalted butter,
at room temperature

14 oz/400 g green beans, trimmed

Freshly cracked black pepper

4 oz/115 g Valtellina Casera or other
mild melting cheese, cut into small cubes

3 fresh rosemary sprigs

Taroz is a very typical dish in Valtellina in northern Italy's Lombardy region, and is one of the most elegant peasant dishes there is. Cooked green beans are mashed together with boiled potatoes; topped with crispy pancetta, caramelized onions, and gooey melted cheese; and finished with melted butter scented with fresh rosemary. Meant as a main course for mountain folk, it is a wonderful accompaniment to roasted pork or goose and grilled trout.

Valtellina Casera is a sweet, mild cheese made from partially skimmed cow's milk, and is a phenomenal melting cheese. Fontina, Bitto, Asiago, and Raclette would all work wonders as well.

Bring a pot of water to a boil over high heat and add a small handful of salt. Add the potatoes and cook until tender but not falling apart, about 12 minutes.

Meanwhile, in a medium skillet over low heat, cook the pancetta until golden and crispy, about 12 minutes. Using a slotted spoon, transfer the pancetta to paper towels to drain. Add the onion and 2 tbsp of the butter to the pan with the pancetta fat. Cook over medium-low heat until the butter is melted and the onion is translucent, about 8 minutes. Raise the heat to high and continue to cook until the onion is caramelized to a rich brown color, 3 to 4 minutes longer. Remove from the heat.

Preheat the broiler. Grease a 6-by-12-in/15-by-30.5-cm ceramic baking dish lightly with butter.

When the potatoes are done, using a slotted spoon, transfer to a large bowl. Add the green beans to the boiling water and cook for 7 to 8 minutes, or until tender. Drain the cooked beans thoroughly in a colander and add to the potatoes. Season well with plenty of salt and pepper. Using a potato masher, mash the potatoes and green beans together until the potatoes are smooth and the beans are broken up and evenly distributed.

Spread the potato–green bean mash in the prepared dish. Scatter the cooked pancetta and onion over the top, followed by the cheese. Wipe any burned bits out of the sauté pan you used to cook the onion and pancetta in, and add the rosemary sprigs and the remaining 2 tbsp butter. Place over medium heat and cook and swirl briefly until the butter is melted and fragrant. Drizzle the scented butter over the casserole and arrange the rosemary sprigs on top. Place the casserole under the broiler until the cheese is melted and golden, 5 to 7 minutes. Serve hot or at room temperature.

BRAISED PORK LOIN SANDWICHES WITH BROCCOLI RABE AND SHARP PROVOLONE

SERVES 4

FOR THE BRAISED PORK:

1 qt/960 ml water

¼ cup/55 g sea salt

2 tbsp sugar

Freshly cracked black pepper

2½ lb/1.2 kg boneless pork loin

1 large shallot, quartered

3 cups/720 ml chicken stock, preferably well-seasoned homemade, or good-quality low-sodium broth

My family and I visit our friends in Philadelphia every year during autumn, when the leaves unleash a riot of harvest colors and the air is crisp and invigorating. Beyond the time spent with friends eating, playing, and swapping parenthood tales, the annual trip is also proof to our Los Angeleno children that there are different seasons.

On our last trip, the other dads kidnapped me and took me to South Philly for a classic sandwich that in my humble opinion blows the socks off of the more famous Philly cheesesteak (whether or not the whiz on that street-food standard can be called cheese is debatable, after all).

Nestled underneath a freeway overpass in the meat-packing district where Rocky tenderized sides of beef with boxing gloves is Tony Luke's, much adored for their take on the "Pork Italian" sandwich. Unbelievably juicy, sweet slices of braised pork shoulder are nestled in a sesame-seed baguette with slightly spicy and bitter sautéed broccoli rabe and melted salty sharp provolone. As they say in Philly: *bee-yoo-de-ful!*

TO MAKE THE BRAISED PORK: Combine the water, salt, sugar, and a few grindings of black pepper in a deep bowl and whisk for several minutes until the salt and sugar dissolve. Add the pork loin and weight it down with a plate topped by a heavy can, if necessary; you want the pork to be completely submerged. Cover and refrigerate for at least 2 hours, or up to 24 hours. Drain, discard the brine, and pat the pork loin dry with paper towels.

Preheat the oven to 400°F/200°C.

Heat a large Dutch oven over medium-high heat. Add the pork loin, fat-side down, and sear for about 5 minutes, or until golden brown. Turn the pork loin, add the shallot, and sear the opposite side for about 5 minutes. Pour the chicken stock into the pot, cover, and place in the oven. Braise until an instant-read thermometer inserted into the thickest part of the pork loin registers 140°F/60°C, 45 to 60 minutes. Remove from the oven and let rest in the juices, still covered, for about 20 minutes.

Bring a medium saucepan of water to a boil over high heat and add a generous pinch or two of salt. Add the broccoli rabe and cook until tender, 6 to 8 minutes. Drain and spread the broccoli rabe out on a cutting board to cool. Chop the cooked broccoli rabe roughly and set aside.

In a large saucepan, heat the olive oil and garlic together over medium heat. Cook, stirring constantly, for about 1 minute, or until the garlic just begins to turn lightly golden, then add the chopped broccoli rabe and the red pepper flakes. Sauté until the broccoli rabe begins to take on some golden edges, 3 to 5 minutes.

To assemble the sandwiches, cut the baguette in half horizontally. Lift the pork loin out of its juices and transfer to a carving board. Using a large, sharp knife, carve into slices against the grain and at a slight angle, as thinly as possible. Arrange the slices evenly on the bottom half of the baguette. Drizzle a little of the cooking juices over the pork loin, then top with the sautéed broccoli rabe. Finally, scatter on the sliced provolone. Replace the top half of baguette, and cut into four sandwiches.

Wrap each sandwich in parchment paper (these are juicy sandwiches) and serve immediately.

Sea salt

1 lb/455 g broccoli rabe, tough stems trimmed

¼ cup/60 ml extra-virgin olive oil

2 or 3 garlic cloves, chopped

¼ tsp red pepper flakes

1 sesame baguette or 4 sesame Italian-style rolls

6 oz/170 g sharp provolone cheese, thinly sliced

WINTER

BELGIAN ENDIVE WITH PISTACHIO OIL, CASHEL BLUE, AND CELERY LEAVES

SERVES 4

2 lemons; halved, 1 cut into wedges

4 large, firm heads Belgian endive

⅓ cup/10 g fresh celery leaves

4 oz/115 g Cashel Blue or other soft blue cheese

Freshly cracked black pepper

2 tbsp pistachio oil

Pistachio oil is one of those luxuries worth splurging on. Kept in the refrigerator, it can last for months, and a little goes a long way, as the fatty oils coat your mouth with the sublime perfume of pistachio. I love to shred leftover chicken, dress it with a drizzle of pistachio oil and some freshly squeezed lime juice, and wrap it up in crisp lettuce leaves.

Indulge in the European tradition of serving salad after the main course, and showcase a really great creamy blue cheese. Cashel Blue from Ireland is one of my all-time favorites.

Squeeze the juice from one lemon half into a bowl and add enough cold water to cover the endive leaves. Core the endives and discard any browned or wilted outer leaves. Separate the remaining leaves by gently pulling them apart, adding them to the bowl of lemon water as you work to keep them from turning brown. Trim the base of the endive as you move closer to the center to loosen the inner leaves. When you reach the firm center and can no longer pull the leaves apart, slice the core thinly and add to the lemon water with the leaves. Drain the endive on a clean kitchen towel and pat dry.

Tear the bigger endive leaves in half and place in a large bowl. Add the celery leaves and squeeze the juice from the remaining lemon half over the salad. Crumble the blue cheese into the bowl and season with plenty of freshly cracked pepper. Toss gently to mix.

Divide the salad among individual plates and drizzle with the pistachio oil. Serve immediately with the lemon wedges.

Escarole is a bitter green we rarely see in salads these days, but on a recent visit to the Bistro du Paradou in Provence, I was blown away by the purity and glory of a large ceramic bowl of pale yellow and green escarole leaves, dressed simply with a fruity local olive oil, some hard-boiled eggs, and beads of very good-quality aged balsamic vinegar. I was hooked immediately.

Point Reyes Blue is an award-winning cheese made by the Giacomini family in Northern California. When the family first introduced their take on blue cheese, many experts speculated that it would become an American classic, and some fourteen years later, it has exceeded all expectations. It is a versatile cheese in the kitchen and, next to Roquefort, is one of the best blues for dressing salads.

Core the escarole and separate the leaves; reserve the large outer leaves for another use.

Soak the tender leaves of the escarole in a large bowl of cold water for 10 minutes, then drain, rinse, drain again, and lay out on clean kitchen towels and pat dry.

In a bowl, combine the blue cheese, crème fraîche, and lemon juice and beat with a fork until creamy and well blended to make a dressing. Season with salt and pepper.

Tear the escarole into bite-size pieces and put in a large serving bowl. Right before serving, peel, halve, and core the pear. Cut into thick slices. Add the pear to the bowl. Crumble the walnuts over the escarole, then add the dressing and toss to coat well. Serve immediately.

ESCAROLE WITH POINT REYES BLUE, PEARS, AND WALNUTS

SERVES 2 TO 4

1 small head escarole

2½ oz/70 g Point Reyes Blue or other blue cheese

6 tbsp/90 ml crème fraîche

3 tbsp fresh lemon juice

Sea salt and freshly cracked black pepper

1 ripe Anjou or Bartlett pear

⅓ cup/45 g walnuts, toasted

BLACK KALE AND PECORINO TOSCANO SALAD WITH TOASTED WALNUTS AND DRIED APRICOTS

SERVES 2 TO 4

6 oz/170 g Tuscan or black kale (cavolo nero), stems and tough center spines removed, leaves thinly sliced

2 oz/55 g dried apricots, roughly chopped

2 oz/55 g walnuts, toasted and roughly chopped

2 oz/55 g Pecorino Toscano or other semi-hard sheep's-milk cheese, cut into shavings with a vegetable peeler or the large slot of a box grater

¼ cup/60 ml fruity extra-virgin olive oil

3 tbsp red wine vinegar

Sea salt and freshly cracked black pepper

Kale has made an amazing comeback since I was a child. Once almost completely relegated to a role as decorative greenery around supermarket meat counters, kale is now widely available in a range of tender European varieties, enjoyed for its intense mineral flavors and superfood health benefits.

This is a bold-flavored salad, with bitter greens, nutty flavors, and sweet dried fruit set against the zing of full-bodied red wine vinegar and extra-virgin olive oil. It's a hearty salad on its own, or serve with a simple white bean salad and cured meats to make antipasti or a picnic.

Put the kale in a large bowl. Add the apricots, walnuts, and Pecorino and toss to mix. Add the olive oil and vinegar, season with salt and pepper, and toss to mix and coat well. Taste and adjust the seasoning. Divide among individual plates and serve immediately.

CRISPY FRIED BRUSSELS SPROUTS WITH PODDA CHEESE AND WARM HONEY

SERVES 4

1 lb/455 g Brussels sprouts

Canola oil for frying

2 oz/55 g Podda cheese, grated

½ cup/170 g light honey

Zest of 2 lemons

Sea salt and freshly cracked black pepper

I simply could not stomach Brussels sprouts when I was a kid. Boiled to death, reeking of sulfur, somehow bitter and bland at the same time; why didn't someone in my family think of frying them?

This is one of my preferred treatments for the little cabbages. Their inherent bitterness works wonders against the sweet warm honey and fantastic Formaggio Podda Classico, a half sheep's-, half cow's-milk grana-style cheese from Sardinia. A good Parmigiano-Reggiano, pecorino, or mix of the two would also work nicely.

Trim the bottoms of the Brussels sprouts and discard, along with any tough or yellowed outer leaves. Separate the remaining leaves, peeling them off until you reach the heart of each sprout. Set the leaves aside; reserve the hearts for another use.

Pour canola oil into a large saucepan to a depth of about 2 in/5 cm and heat to 350°F/180°C on a deep-frying thermometer. Working in batches to avoid crowding the pan, fry the sprout leaves for about 30 seconds, or until the leaves are golden and crisp. Using a slotted spoon or a wire skimmer, transfer to paper towels to drain. Sprinkle the leaves with some of the cheese while they are still warm.

In a small saucepan over medium-low heat, warm the honey.

When all the leaves are fried and sprinkled with cheese, transfer to a serving bowl and toss with the lemon zest and season with salt and pepper. Drizzle with the warm honey. Serve immediately.

Saba, the southern Italian word for cooked grape must, is made from sweet unfermented grape juice that is slowly cooked in copper pots to about one-third its original volume. It is a deep, dense syrup that some call the "honey of the grapes." It can be drizzled over fresh ricotta or strong, aged pecorino; dripped onto vanilla bean–studded panna cotta; or brushed on roasted vegetables and even roasted birds like chicken or duck.

Saba is a luxury item to those of us not living on or near a vineyard, but a little goes a very long way and it keeps well in a cool dark place, perhaps next to your bottles of Mugolio pine syrup (see page 56) and white truffle oil!

In a large sauté pan or skillet, heat 1 tbsp of the olive oil over medium-high heat until hot but not smoking. Add about one-fourth of the sliced squash, laying each slice flat in the pan to sear. Season with salt and pepper. Cook for about 2 minutes, or until deep golden with little brown spots on one side. Turn the slices and cook for about 2 minutes longer, or until each side is golden and the squash is tender but not falling apart. Transfer to paper towels to drain.

Repeat to cook the remaining squash slices with olive oil in three more batches. Set aside.

Wipe the pan clean and return to medium-high heat. Without adding any extra oil and working in batches as needed to avoid crowding the pan, toast the pieces of baguette on both sides until crisp, about 2 minutes per side. Remove from the heat and cool.

Arrange the toasted baguette slices on a serving dish. Lay one slice of the squash atop each slice of baguette, folding over as necessary to fit. Crumble the cheese and scatter atop the squash, dividing it evenly. Anoint each slice with just a couple drops of the *saba* (a small demitasse spoon works wonders for this) and serve immediately.

FRIED BANANA SQUASH CROSTINI WITH CAÑA DE CABRA AND SABA

MAKES 36 CROSTINI; SERVES 8 TO 12

4 tbsp/60 ml extra-virgin olive oil

One 1-lb/455-g chunk banana squash, peeled, halved, and seeded, flesh cut into 36 slices about ⅛ in/3 mm thick

Sea salt and freshly cracked black pepper

½ baguette, cut into 36 slices ¼ in/6 mm thick

4 oz/110 g Caña de Cabra or other soft-ripened goat- or sheep's-milk cheese

2 to 4 tbsp *saba*

MELTED VACHERIN WITH ORGANIC FARM CARROTS

SERVES 4 TO 6

One 1-lb/455-g wheel Vacherin Mont d'Or or Camembert cheese, in its wooden box

2 tsp good-quality kirsch

4 or 5 large organic carrots, peeled and cut into sticks

The smiling face of Jerry Rutiz can be found every week at the wildly popular farmers' market in Santa Monica, California. While his local farm produces a good variety of vegetables, it's their carrots I love the most.

These are big, fat carrots, at least 2 in/5 cm thick, that would likely be considered ugly by their slim, sexy supermarket counterparts. But what these carrots lack in glamour, they more than make up for in sugary-sweet flavor. With a glug of olive oil in a hot oven, they roast like magic, and are a fantastic crunchy snack or appetizer dipped in hot and funky melted cheese.

Vacherin Mont d'Or is a decadent, creamy cow's-milk cheese aged in pinewood boxes from the French Alps. Melting Vacherin is less about cooking the cheese and more about gently warming it to bring out every little nuance. While boiled potatoes are traditional with this preparation, the sweetness and crunch of raw carrots are great contrast to the rich cheese and a delightful way to begin or end a winter meal.

Preheat the oven to 400°F/200°C.

If there is a plastic or paper wrapping around the cheese inside the box, remove it and discard. Place the cheese back in the box. Using a wooden skewer or fork, poke several holes in the surface of the cheese.

Sprinkle the kirsch over the holes and cover the cheese with the lid to the box, or with aluminum foil if the cheese was sold without its lid. Bake for 15 to 20 minutes, or until the cheese is melted and hot throughout.

Place the hot cheese on a nice wood cutting board or serving plate and surround it with the carrot sticks. Serve immediately in the center of the table, allowing friends and family to scoop up the cheese with the carrot sticks.

Pecorino Moliterno is a sheep's-milk cheese from Sardinia that is injected with black truffle paste. Unlike many truffle-infused cheeses, Moliterno is allowed to mature on its own before the truffles are added, resulting in a cheese tasting that is first a complex pecorino, followed right behind by the perfume of the truffle. Moliterno is both a grand table cheese and fantastic shaved over many foods, from grilled asparagus to fried eggs. Substitute other truffle-infused cheeses for this recipe, or even a non-truffle, aged pecorino.

Using a sharp knife, vegetable peeler, or mandoline, slice the cauliflower florets as thinly as possible. Some will crumble as you slice, but don't worry, this leaves a nice mixture of crosscut slices and smaller, broken pieces.

Gently transfer the cauliflower to a bowl and add the cheese, olive oil, and parsley and season with salt and a few grindings of pepper. Toss gently to mix. Taste and adjust the seasoning. (Remember that the pecorino will add quite a bit of the salt needed.) Transfer to individual plates and serve at room temperature.

RAW CAULIFLOWER SALAD WITH BLACK-TRUFFLE PECORINO

SERVES 4

1 head cauliflower, cored, trimmed, and cut into 1- to 2-in/2.5- to 5-cm florets

3 oz/85 g Pecorino Moliterno or other truffle-infused pecorino

¼ cup/60 ml extra-virgin olive oil

¼ cup/7 g fresh flat-leaf (Italian) parsley leaves

Sea salt and freshly cracked black pepper

CAULIFLOWER PURÉE WITH CANTAL

SERVES 4

1 large head cauliflower

1½ cups/360 ml water

1 cup/240 ml whole milk

Sea salt

2 tbsp unsalted butter, at room temperature

6 oz/170 g Cantal, Gruyère, or aged Cheddar cheese, shredded

Freshly cracked black pepper

I recently discovered a magnificent pork porterhouse at my friendly neighborhood artisanal butcher. Yes, the pork loin and the pork tenderloin of locally raised pigs, together in one chop!

Simply grilled with a few slices of garlic, some fresh oregano from the garden, and plenty of salt and pepper, this monster cut of meat needed only one thing to send it over the top: a silky, creamy bed of puréed cauliflower with grated Cantal cheese, my go-to accompaniment for grilled pork. It's an elegant replacement for mashed potatoes, with a delicate texture that is phenomenal with the leaner cuts of pork and chicken.

Core the cauliflower and cut into small florets. (Save the stalk and stems you trim off; they're delicious for snacking while cooking, sliced and dressed with a glug of extra-virgin olive oil and plenty of flaky sea salt.)

Place the florets in a medium saucepan along with the water and milk. Season with plenty of salt and bring to a boil over high heat. Reduce the heat to a simmer and cook until the cauliflower is very tender but not mushy, about 10 minutes.

Drain the cauliflower, reserving ½ cup/120 ml of the cooking liquid. Transfer the cauliflower to a food processor fitted with the blade attachment. Add the butter, cheese, and about half of the reserved cooking liquid and pulse just until a smooth purée is formed. Add more of the cooking liquid, a little at a time, if needed. The purée should be slightly looser than mashed potatoes. Season well with salt and pepper. Serve immediately.

CARAMELIZED SHALLOT AND BLEU D'AUVERGNE TARTLETS WITH CHERRY BLOSSOM HONEY

MAKES FIFTEEN 2-IN/5-CM TARTLETS

3 tbsp extra-virgin olive oil

About 1 lb/455 g shallots, broken up into small to medium cloves

¼ cup/50 g sugar

1 cup/240 ml water

Sea salt and freshly cracked black pepper

One 10-by-15-in/25-by-38-cm sheet puff pastry

9 oz/255 g Bleu d'Auvergne or other soft blue cheese

Cherry blossom or wildflower honey for drizzling

Bleu d'Auvergne is a creamy cow's-milk blue cheese from central France, a welcome variety on many cheeseboards for its sweet, buttery flavors. Made in a similar style to sheep's-milk Roquefort, it is less salty and much higher in fat, and therefore is a wonderful cheese to work with in the kitchen.

These are delightful little appetizers, packed full of flavor. The shallots, sweet from being cooked in sugar, contrast against the warm blue cheese, and the fragrance of cherry blossom honey ties the flavors together most wonderfully.

Heat the olive oil in a large sauté pan or skillet over medium-high heat until hot but not smoking. Add the shallots and sauté for about 5 minutes, or until lightly browned on all sides. Sprinkle the sugar over the shallots and cook for 1 minute longer, then add the water slowly, taking care not to get splattered with the hot oil. Season well with salt and pepper.

Reduce the heat to maintain a gentle simmer and cook, stirring often, until the shallots are caramelized to a rich brown color and easily pierced with the tip of a sharp knife, and a rich, thick syrup has formed, about 20 minutes. Remove from the heat and let cool in their liquid. (The caramelized shallots can be made to this point up to 1 day in advance and refrigerated until ready to use.)

Preheat the oven to 425°F/220°C.

Cut the puff pastry into fifteen 2½-by-2-in/ 6-by-5-cm pieces and lay them out on a baking sheet lined with parchment paper.

Crumble the cheese and divide evenly among the centers of the pastry squares. Cut each of the caramelized shallots in half and divide them atop the cheese on each pastry.

Bake for 12 to 15 minutes, or until the pastry is golden and cooked through. If any shallots slide out of place, push them back into the center of the tartlets with a fork.

Transfer to a wire rack and let cool slightly. Serve warm with a drizzle of honey.

I'm a big fan of eating fennel raw, especially when it's dipped in high-quality extra-virgin olive oil with a sprinkle of flaky sea salt. I also enjoy the more subtle flavors of braised fennel. Using chicken stock or lightly salted water, once the fennel is cooked but still firm, it can be drained and seared until golden in a hot pan with a brush of olive oil, or topped with a decadent truffle-infused cheese and baked until bubbly. Fennel, truffles, and cheese are a great combination with pork. And nowhere do they know pork better than Umbria.

Caciotta al Tartufo is a tangy, semisoft cheese made with a mixture of sheep's and cow's milk and studded with black truffles from Umbria. Since the truffle flavors explode when heated, this cheese is perfect melted on pizzas or baked with vegetables and pasta. A version from Tuscany known as Boschetto al Tartufo and even a milder truffle cheese like Sottocenere from the Veneto can be found quite easily these days, and would work well. The fennel is a superb accompaniment to roasted chicken or grilled fish.

Preheat the oven to 400°F/200°C. Grease an 11-by-8-in/28-by-20-cm ceramic baking dish with the butter. Add 2 tbsp of the bread crumbs, tilt the pan to coat, and tap out the excess.

Bring a pot of salted water to a boil. Meanwhile, core the fennel bulbs and cut into slices about ¼ in/6 mm thick. Add the fennel to the boiling water and cook until tender but still firm, 5 to 6 minutes, then drain well and transfer to a large bowl.

Add 3 tbsp of the olive oil to the fennel and season with salt and pepper. Pour the seasoned fennel into the prepared baking dish and spread out evenly. Scatter the Caciotta al Tartufo cheese over the top, followed by the Grana Padano and then the remaining 2 tbsp bread crumbs. Sprinkle the minced fennel fronds on top, then drizzle with the remaining 3 tbsp olive oil.

Bake for 20 minutes, or until the cheeses are melted, bubbly, and golden brown. Serve hot or at room temperature.

FENNEL GRATIN WITH CACIOTTA AL TARTUFO

SERVES 6

1 tbsp unsalted butter, at room temperature

4 tbsp/30 g dried bread crumbs

Sea salt

2 or 3 fennel bulbs, fronds and stems removed, plus 2 tbsp minced fronds

6 tbsp/90 ml extra-virgin olive oil

Freshly cracked black pepper

8 oz/225 g Caciotta al Tartufo, Sottocenere, or other truffle-infused semi-soft cheese, shredded

2 oz/55 g Grana Padano or Parmigiano-Reggiano cheese, grated

CANNELLINI BEANS WITH SAGE AND PARMIGIANO-REGGIANO

SERVES 6

1 lb/455 g dried cannellini beans

1 small yellow onion, halved through the root end

1 celery stalk, broken in half

5 fresh sage leaves

¼ cup/60 ml extra-virgin olive oil

3 garlic cloves, peeled but left whole

Juice of 1 lemon

4 oz/115 g Parmigiano-Reggiano cheese, broken up into small shards

Sea salt and freshly cracked black pepper

Cannellini beans are at the top of my list of comfort foods. In this recipe, they are cooked to tenderness and anointed with fruity oil, fresh herbs, and shards of Parmigiano-Reggiano.

Serve the bean salad at room temperature; spoon it into cups of raw radicchio leaves for a pretty presentation. It is also delightful on a picnic along with cold grilled chicken spiced with crushed chiles.

High-quality cooked beans are available in fine food stores and convenient to have in the pantry. But a little foresight and very little work can provide you with a wonderful homemade result that is well worth it.

Sort through the beans and discard any small stones. Rinse the beans in a colander under cold running water, drain, and put them in a pot. Add water to cover by 2 in/5 cm. Soak for at least 6 hours, or preferably overnight.

Drain the soaked beans and return them to the pot. Add 3 qt/2.8 L fresh cold water, the onion, celery, and 2 of the sage leaves. Cover and bring to a simmer over medium-high heat. Reduce the heat to medium-low and simmer for 45 minutes to 1 hour, or until the beans are quite tender to the bite but not mushy.

Drain the beans well and spread out on a baking sheet to cool to room temperature. Discard the onion, celery, and sage leaves. (The beans can be prepared to this point and kept, tightly covered, in the refrigerator for up to 2 days.)

Heat the olive oil in a large sauté pan or skillet over medium heat until hot but not smoking. Add the garlic cloves and cook, turning once or twice, until golden brown on both sides. Add the remaining 3 sage leaves and fry until crispy, about 1 minute. Add the cooked beans and stir to coat with the fragrant oil. Raise the heat to high and sauté the beans for 1 minute, then transfer to a large bowl. Add the lemon juice and Parmigiano shards and toss well. Season with salt and pepper and serve at room temperature. Leftover beans will keep covered in the refrigerator for 2 days.

TUSCAN WHITE BEANS AND CORN-MEAL WITH CAVOLO NERO AND PIAVE (FARINATA)

SERVES 6 TO 8

8 oz/225 g dried cannellini beans

2 garlic cloves

3 large fresh sage leaves

4 tbsp/60 ml peppery extra-virgin olive oil, such as Tuscan

3 oz/85 g pancetta, chopped

2 medium yellow onions, chopped

Many visitors to Liguria will be familiar with the fried chick-pea and olive oil cake called *farinata*. This dish from neighboring Tuscany bears the same name, but that is where the similarities end.

Tuscan *farinata* is a hearty, although somehow not too heavy, porridge of black cabbage cooked with white beans and cornmeal—a kind of gardener's polenta—and is often served as a main course with a goodly drizzle of the famous peppery olive oil from the same region. Not always made with cheese, I have taken the liberty of adding the mild Piave to this peasant dish, where it works wonders. Grana Padano or Parmigiano-Reggiano would be great substitutes.

Farinata can be served hot as soon as it is cooked, or spread out on a baking tray and allowed to cool, then sliced into squares and fried or grilled.

Sort through the beans and discard any small stones. Rinse the beans in a colander under cold running water, drain, and put them in a pot. Add water to cover by 2 in/5 cm. Soak for at least 6 hours, or preferably overnight.

Drain the soaked beans and return them to the pot along with the garlic cloves and sage leaves. Add 12 cups fresh cold water. Cover and bring to a boil over high heat. Reduce the heat to low and simmer for 45 minutes to 1 hour, or until the beans are tender to the bite but not falling apart. Remove from the heat. Using a slotted spoon or wire-mesh strainer, transfer half of the beans to a bowl. Mash with a fork and set aside. Strain the cooking liquid from the remaining beans into a bowl; set the liquid and the whole beans aside separately.

Meanwhile, in a large deep-sided sauté pan, heat 1 tbsp of the olive oil over medium heat. Add the pancetta and cook, stirring occasionally, until it just begins to crisp, about 5 minutes. Add the onions and stir to coat well with the oil and melted pancetta fat. Continue cooking and stirring over medium heat until the onions are translucent, about 10 minutes.

Add the tomatoes, the mashed beans, the whole beans, and the bean-cooking water plus fresh water to equal a total of 9 cups/2.1 L. Season with salt and pepper and simmer to allow the flavors to blend, about 5 minutes.

Add the kale, reduce the heat to low, and cook, stirring occasionally, for 10 minutes, or until the kale is tender. At this point, add the cornmeal in a slow and steady stream, stirring constantly with a wooden spoon to prevent lumps. Continue stirring constantly until the mixture begins to thicken, about 5 minutes.

Meanwhile, fill the bottom pan of a double boiler with about 2 in/5 cm of water and bring to a boil over high heat. Reduce the heat to maintain a gentle simmer, and scrape the contents of the sauté pan into the top pan of the double boiler. Nest the top pan over the simmering water, cover, and cook the *farinata* for 30 minutes. Uncover, stir well, re-cover, and continue cooking for another 30 minutes, or until the cornmeal is cooked and creamy.

If the *farinata* seems too thick, bring a little water to a boil and add a ladleful or two as needed to thin it; it should be the texture of creamy porridge. Divide among warmed individual bowls. Top with the grated Piave and drizzle with the remaining 3 tbsp olive oil. Serve hot.

1 lb/455 g ripe tomatoes, peeled, seeded, and chopped, or one 28-oz/800-g can plum (Roma) tomatoes, preferably San Marzano, drained, seeded, and chopped

Sea salt and freshly cracked black pepper

1 lb/455 g Tuscan or black kale (cavolo nero), stems and tough center spines removed, leaves thinly sliced

2 cups/400 g coarse-ground cornmeal or polenta

6 oz/170 g Piave cheese, grated

ORECCHIETTE WITH CHICKPEAS, PECORINO CROTONESE, AND RED CHILE

SERVES 4

1¼ cups/255 g dried chickpeas, or one
14-oz/400-g can chickpeas, drained and rinsed

12 oz/340 g dried orecchiette

Sea salt

3 tbsp extra-virgin olive oil

1 medium yellow onion, chopped

3 garlic cloves

1 tsp chopped fresh rosemary

A Calabrian once proudly described his region in southern Italy as "the Mexico of Italy," in reference to the prolific use of spicy chiles to cool the body in a hot and dry land. The analogy goes further, since both cultures display proud identities amidst a sometimes hostile environment in terms of crime as well as climate, and both have rich traditions of colorful costumes and celebrations with food.

Pecorino Crotonese originally comes from its namesake, the Calabrian town of Crotone, although there are increasingly good imitations of the cheese being made to the west, on the island of Sardinia. Aged anywhere from 2 to 18 months, the young to mid-aged wheels have a sweet sheep's-milk flavor that is not overpowered by saltiness. It is a delightful table and even dessert cheese, and marries wonderfully with nutty chickpeas and fiery chiles. If using a dried chile, use one that is not too dry, both for ease of slicing and for the crisp flavor.

If using dried chickpeas, sort through them and discard any small stones. Rinse the chickpeas in a colander under cold running water, drain, and put them in a pot. Add water to cover by 2 in/5 cm. Soak for at least 6 hours, or preferably overnight.

Drain the soaked chickpeas and return them to the pot. Add 3 qt/2.8 L fresh cold water. Cover and bring to a boil over high heat. Reduce the heat to low and simmer for 45 minutes to 1 hour, or until the chickpeas are tender to the bite but not falling apart. Drain well and set aside.

Bring a large pot of water to a boil over high heat. Add the orecchiette, along with a small handful of salt. Cook, stirring occasionally, until al dente, about 5 minutes.

Ladle about ½ cup/120 ml of the pasta-cooking water into the chickpea mixture. Drain the pasta, reserving 1 cup/240 ml of the cooking water, and transfer to a large serving bowl.

Meanwhile, heat the olive oil in a large sauté pan or skillet over medium-high heat. Add the onion and garlic and cook, stirring often, until the onion is translucent and the garlic is lightly golden, about 5 minutes. Add the rosemary and chile and sauté for about 1 minute, or until fragrant. Stir in the chopped tomato, chickpeas (cooked or canned), and ½ cup/120 ml of the pasta cooking water. Season with plenty of salt and black pepper. Bring to a simmer and cook for 5 minutes.

Using a fork, mash about half of the chickpeas in the pan and stir to create a thick and rich sauce. Pour the chickpea sauce into the bowl with the pasta and add about half of the Pecorino. Add a spoonful or two of the reserved pasta-cooking water if the dish seems too dry. Scatter the remaining Pecorino over the top of the pasta and serve immediately.

1 small fresh or dried red chile, thinly sliced crosswise, or ½ tsp red pepper flakes

1 medium ripe tomato, peeled, seeded, and chopped

Freshly cracked black pepper

6 oz/170 g Pecorino Crotonese or other aged sheep's-milk cheese, grated

CASTELFRANCO RADICCHIO WITH APPLES, SAN DANIELE PROSCIUTTO, AND UBRIACO AL PROSECCO

SERVES 4 TO 6

2 heads Castelfranco radicchio

2 Pink Lady or other sweet, crisp apples

1 tbsp fresh lemon juice

2 oz/55 g Prosciutto di San Daniele or other high-quality prosciutto, thinly sliced

3 tbsp extra-virgin olive oil

1 tbsp red wine vinegar

Sea salt and freshly cracked black pepper

3 oz/85 g Ubriaco al Prosecco or Grana Padano, cut into shavings with a vegetable peeler or the large slot of a box grater

This salad highlights three special ingredients from the Veneto area: gorgeous, pale green and red-speckled radicchio known as Castelfranco; sweet and savory Prosciutto di San Daniele; and Ubriaco al Prosecco, an aged raw cow's-milk cheese rubbed with the skins of the white grapes used for Prosecco.

Castelfranco is an heirloom winter green that is much less peppery than the red Chioggia and Treviso varieties of radicchio. A mixture of butter (Boston) lettuce and escarole would be a nice substitution if Castelfranco is unavailable.

Core the radicchio, tear the leaves into large pieces, and rinse and dry well. Place the leaves in a large serving bowl. Peel and core the apples, then cut in half. Cut each half into thin slices and toss in a small bowl with the lemon juice to keep them from turning brown. Add the apple slices to the radicchio. Tear the prosciutto into small, uneven pieces and add to the salad.

In a small bowl, whisk together the olive oil and vinegar and season with salt and pepper to make a vinaigrette. Taste and adjust the seasoning. Add to the salad and toss to mix well. Scatter on the cheese and toss again. Divide among individual plates and serve immediately.

SHREDDED RADICCHIO SALAD WITH CASATICA, BACON, AND CHERRY BLOSSOM HONEY DRESSING

SERVES 4

4 slices high-quality smoked bacon, chopped

2 small heads Chioggia radicchio

¼ cup/60 ml extra-virgin olive oil

2 tbsp cherry blossom or wildflower honey

2 tbsp fresh lemon juice

Sea salt and freshly cracked black pepper

8 oz/225 g Casatica cheese

Alfio and Bruno Gritti introduced water buffalo to their father's dairy near Bergamo in northern Italy over a decade ago, and the results are stupendous. Water buffalo's milk is very rich in cream (it has twice that of regular cow's milk), and can be made into many kinds of cheese beyond the famous mozzarella di bufala. In fact, the brothers Gritti are responsible for the incredible Blu di Bufala cheese that I love so dearly.

Casatica is another Gritti creation from their water buffalo husbandry, a soft-ripened, creamy, bone-white cheese. It has a thin, edible rind and is milky sweet. Here, the creaminess is contrasted with the bitter crunch of raw radicchio, the smoky depth of crispy bacon, and the delicate essence of a cherry blossom honey dressing. Stracchino or Taleggio would also work well here.

In a small skillet over medium-high heat, cook the bacon until crispy, about 5 minutes. Transfer to paper towels to drain and set aside.

Cut the radicchio heads in half. Using the tip of the knife, cut out the core from each half and discard. Turn the radicchio onto the board, cut-side down, and slice very thinly. Transfer the shredded radicchio to a large bowl.

In a small bowl, whisk together the olive oil, honey, and lemon juice and season with salt and pepper to make a dressing. Taste and adjust the seasoning.

Tear the Casatica into small bite-size pieces and add to the bowl with the radicchio. Add the dressing and toss well to combine. Pile the salad onto individual plates, dividing it evenly, and scatter the crispy bacon over the top. Serve immediately.

RISOTTO WITH RADICCHIO, BRESCIANELLA, AND AMARONE

SERVES 4 TO 6

6 cups/1.4 L chicken stock, homemade or good-quality low-sodium purchased

8 tbsp/110 g unsalted butter, at room temperature

1 medium yellow onion, finely chopped

2 cups/400 g Carnaroli or Arborio rice

¾ cup/180 ml Amarone wine

1 head Chioggia radicchio, cored and shredded

1 cup/200 g freshly grated Grana Padano or Parmigiano-Reggiano cheese

Sea salt and freshly cracked black pepper

6 oz/170 g Brescianella or Taleggio cheese

An Italian proverb says, "Rice is born in water and dies in wine." In this case, it's a death with a heavenly afterlife.

Amarone is made in Valpolicella north of Verona, where the grapes are actually allowed to dry halfway to raisins before being pressed, thereby concentrating not only the dried fruit flavors, but creating a wine much higher in alcohol. While it may seem a touch extravagant to use such a noble wine for cooking, like the famous risotto with Barolo, this dish is a celebration of the wine's power and depth.

Brescianella is a soft, washed-rind cow's-milk cheese from Lombardy—a creamy, slightly saltier and nuttier cousin to Taleggio. It is a cheese that does not want to be cooked, but rather gently warmed by the heat of the underlying rice. For this dish, if your cheese is not overly ripe, eat the rind, too, as its slight funkiness is countered perfectly by the bitter crunch of the radicchio and the bold flavors in a splash of Amarone, which I like to drizzle straight from the wine bottle or decanter over guests' plates at the table.

In a saucepan, warm the stock over medium heat until hot. Reduce the heat to medium-low and keep the pan on a nearby burner while you cook the risotto.

Melt 4 tbsp/55 g of the butter in a large sauté pan or skillet over medium heat. Add the onion and cook until translucent, about 5 minutes. Add the rice all at once and stir, being sure to coat all the grains with the butter. Cook for about 5 minutes, stirring constantly, or until the outside layer of the rice grains becomes translucent. Add ¼ cup/60 ml of the wine and stir until completely absorbed, 2 to 3 minutes longer.

Begin adding the hot stock, one ladleful at a time, stirring constantly. As the stock is absorbed, continue adding more, all the while striking a balance between keeping the rice undulating but not swimming in liquid.

After 15 or 20 minutes, the rice should be cooked, with a nice chew but not crunchy. Remove from the heat and add the radicchio, the remaining 4 tbsp/55 g butter, and the Grana Padano, stirring well to create an ultra-creamy risotto. Season with salt and plenty of freshly cracked pepper.

Pour the risotto into a warmed large serving bowl or divide among warmed individual bowls. Distribute the Brescianella in slices or chunks over the hot rice and anoint each serving with the remaining ½ cup/120 ml wine, dividing it evenly. Serve immediately.

POPPY SEED FETTUCCINE WITH RADICCHIO, SAUSAGE, AND PUZZONE DI MOENA

SERVES 4 TO 6

FOR THE PASTA DOUGH:

2 cups/255 g all-purpose flour

3 large eggs

1 tbsp poppy seeds

Sea salt

Puzzone di Moena is a washed-rind raw cow's-milk cheese from the Alto Adige in northern Italy. Literally meaning "stinky," Puzzone is indeed a pungent cheese, especially when melted, a characteristic that balances wonderfully with the bitterness of wilted radicchio and sausage on this uber-elegant poppy seed pasta. Fontina or Crucolo would be a nice substitute.

TO MAKE THE PASTA DOUGH: Put the flour in a bowl and make a well in the center. Break the eggs into the center of the well and add the poppy seeds. Using a fork, beat the eggs until well blended. Continue beating, and begin to pull flour from the sides of the well a little at a time. Gradually add more flour from the well to the mix as you work, until all of the flour is incorporated and a sticky dough forms.

Turn the dough out onto a generously floured work surface and knead, adding more flour as needed to prevent sticking, until the dough is soft and supple, about 5 minutes. Roll the dough into a ball and wrap tightly with plastic wrap. Let rest at room temperature for 1 hour.

Unwrap the dough and cut in half. Return one half to the plastic wrap and keep covered. Cut the other piece of dough in half again. Run one dough piece through a pasta machine with the rollers at the widest setting. Repeat, and then roll the dough twice through each successively narrower setting, until you have a sheet about 1/16 in/2 mm thick, or even a little thinner. As you work, dust your hands, the rollers, and the dough lightly with flour as needed to prevent sticking, and lay the finished sheet on a lightly floured work surface. Repeat with the second dough piece, then unwrap and repeat the whole process with the second half of the dough, for four sheets. Attach the cutting blade to the pasta machine and cut the sheets into fettuccine. Sprinkle the noodles with a small amount of flour to keep them from sticking and spread out on a clean, dry kitchen towel or piece of parchment.

cont'd

FOR THE SAUCE:

3 tbsp extra-virgin olive oil

1 small red onion, halved lengthwise and thinly sliced crosswise

8 oz/225 g sweet Italian sausage, casings removed

1 large head Chioggia radicchio, cored and thinly sliced

Sea salt and freshly cracked black pepper

¼ cup/60 ml dry red wine

6 tbsp/85 g unsalted butter, at room temperature

7 oz/200 g Puzzone di Moena cheese, cut into small cubes, at room temperature

4 oz/115 g Parmigiano-Reggiano, grated, plus more for serving (optional)

Bring a large pot of water to a boil over high heat and add a small handful of salt.

WHILE THE WATER IS HEATING, MAKE THE SAUCE: Heat the olive oil in a large sauté pan or skillet over medium-high heat. Add the onion and cook until translucent, about 5 minutes. Add the sausage and break it up with a fork. Cook, stirring occasionally, for about 10 minutes, or until the sausage is cooked through and nicely browned. Pour off a small amount of fat from the pan, then add the radicchio and return to medium-high heat, stirring well to combine with the sausage and onion. Season with salt and pepper. Raise the heat to high and sauté for 1 minute.

Add the wine and stir, scraping up any browned bits from the bottom of the pan. Continue cooking over high heat for 1 minute, or until the wine reduces and thickens into the sauce, then remove from the heat and pour the sauce into a large serving bowl.

Add the pasta to the boiling water and cook for 1 minute, or until al dente. Drain well, reserving about ½ cup/120 ml of the cooking water. Add the butter and Puzzone to the bowl with the sauce, then add the hot cooked pasta and stir well to combine and melt the cheese. Add a few spoonfuls of the pasta-cooking water if the sauce seems too dry. Scatter the Parmigiano over the top along with plenty of freshly cracked pepper. Serve immediately, with more Parmigiano, if desired.

BUCKWHEAT PASTA WITH SAVOY CABBAGE, POTATOES, AND BITTO (PIZZOCCHERI)

SERVES 4 TO 6

FOR THE PASTA DOUGH:

2 cups/200 g buckwheat flour

1 cup/130 g all-purpose flour

1 cup/240 ml lukewarm water

From the Valtellina Valley in northern Italy's Lombardy region comes this provincial classic dish rarely seen outside of Italy. Fresh buckwheat pasta is tossed with wilted savoy cabbage, tender potatoes, Fontina cheese, and loads of butter—in fact, traditionally this hearty peasant dish calls for far more butter than most of us can imagine, as it is a dish intended to pack calories into the body for working in the cold snow-filled mountains.

By reducing the amount of butter considerably, and dividing the portions into smaller sizes among more people, the heart-warming flavors of this unique Italian dish can be savored and enjoyed by us non-mountain folk, and are ideal in the cold winter months.

Buckwheat pasta dough is much more delicate to work with than dough for typical fresh egg pasta, and pizzoccheri (the shape of noodle the dough is cut into) are meant to be a bit thicker than egg noodles, so handle the dough gently and resist the temptation to roll the noodles any thinner than called for here. You can substitute purchased Japanese soba noodles, although the characteristic density of pizzoccheri will be lost.

While Fontina is the cheese most commonly used for this dish, if you can find a wheel of Bitto at your local cheesemonger, I highly recommend it. Made in the same region as Fontina, Bitto cheese is made of cow's milk and a small amount of goat's milk. Its flavor is filled with notes of mountain grass and wildflowers, and is amazing when melted.

TO MAKE THE PASTA DOUGH: Sift both flours together into a medium bowl. Add the water and stir until combined, then flour your hands and knead gently in the bowl until a soft and silky dough forms. (If the dough does not come together smoothly, knead in a splash more lukewarm water.) Form the dough into a ball, wrap in plastic wrap, and let rest for 30 minutes.

Unwrap the dough and cut in half. Return one half to the plastic wrap and keep covered. Run the other dough piece through a pasta machine with the rollers at the widest setting. Repeat, and then roll the dough twice through each successively narrower setting, until you have a sheet about ⅜ in/ 1 cm thick. As you work, dust your hands, the rollers, and the dough lightly with flour as needed to pre-vent sticking, and lay the finished sheet on a lightly floured work surface. Repeat with the second dough piece. Using the tip of a sharp knife, cut into noodles about 2 in/5 cm wide and 5 in/12 cm long. Spread the noodles out and dust lightly with flour to keep them from sticking.

Bring a large pot of water to a boil over high heat and add a small handful of salt. Reduce the heat to medium-high, add the potato, and cook until tender, about 10 minutes. Using a wire-mesh strainer, trans-fer the potato to a plate. Add the cabbage to the water and cook for 6 to 7 minutes, or until tender, then remove with the strainer and pile next to the potato on the plate. Set aside.

Bring the water back to a boil, adding more to the pot if the level has dropped below halfway full. Add the pasta, stir once to prevent sticking, and cook for about 4 minutes, or until al dente. Drain in a colander.

While the pasta is cooking, warm a 6-by-12-in/15-by-30.5-cm ceramic serving dish in a low oven. In a medium sauté pan or skillet, melt the butter over low heat, then add the garlic and sage leaves. Cook until the garlic is fragrant and the sage is just beginning to crisp, about 3 minutes. Remove from the heat.

Spread half of the cooked pasta in the bottom of the warmed dish. Scatter on half of the cabbage, half of the potato, and then half of both cheeses. Repeat to make another layer of pasta, cabbage, potato, and cheese. Season with salt and black pep-per. Pour the melted butter over the dish evenly, including the sage leaves and garlic pieces. Serve hot, mixing the entire dish at the table as you plate.

Sea salt

1 large russet potato, peeled and cut into small cubes

½ to 1 small head savoy cabbage, cored and roughly chopped

½ cup/110 g unsalted butter

4 garlic cloves, slightly smashed

12 fresh sage leaves

7 oz/200 g Bitto or Fontina cheese, cut into small cubes

3 oz/85 g Parmigiano-Reggiano cheese, grated

Freshly cracked black pepper

SPINACH CRESPELLE WITH PARMIGIANO CREAM AND TOMA

MAKES 10 CRESPELLE; SERVES 4 OR 5

FOR THE CRESPELLE:

2 large eggs

1 tbsp extra-virgin olive oil, plus more for greasing

1 cup/240 ml milk

½ cup/65 g all-purpose flour

¼ tsp sea salt

My wife and I spent our seven-year anniversary in Point Reyes, California. It was a magical escape from the chaos of city living, with days spent wandering the windswept beaches and green dairy hills, and evenings discovering old-time barn dances and locals celebrating the simple life.

In addition to the artisanal cheese mecca that is Cowgirl Creamery, we paid an unannounced visit to the Point Reyes Farmstead Cheese Company, where the Giacomini family has reinvented the great American blue cheese with their award-winning Point Reyes Blue.

While poking around the dairy, in sheer awe at the spotlessly clean herd of more than three hundred Holsteins, we were greeted by none other than Bob Giacomini himself, who personally took us around and showed us his amazing operation. Afterward, he insisted on giving us a rather large wedge of one of their lesser-known cheeses: Toma, a classic Italian-style semihard cow's-milk cheese with a creamy texture and buttery, tangy flavor that is versatile in the kitchen. When melted, it has a texture like Monterey Jack, but it is eminently more flavorful.

TO MAKE THE CRESPELLE: In a bowl, combine the eggs, the 1 tbsp olive oil, the milk, flour, and salt and whisk until well mixed. Cover and let stand at room temperature for 1 hour.

Heat a 10-in/25-cm skillet over medium heat. Wipe the hot pan with a paper towel dipped in a small amount of olive oil to grease the pan.

Pour 3 tbsp of the batter into a small bowl or measuring cup and then pour it all at once into the hot pan, swirling to coat the pan bottom evenly with the batter. Return to the heat and cook for about 1 minute, or until the sides begin to turn a light golden brown. Loosen the edges of the crespelle with the tip of a metal spatula, then carefully turn the crespelle over and cook for another minute. Turn the crespelle out onto a clean plate, wipe the pan with the oiled paper towel, and repeat to make nine more crespelle.

Heat a large sauté pan or skillet over high heat. Add the spinach with whatever water is still clinging to the leaves and cook until all of the leaves are wilted, using a pair of tongs to help move the spinach around. Transfer to a colander to let stand until cool enough to handle. Squeeze the spinach with your hands to get out as much water as possible and set aside.

Preheat the oven to 400°F/200°C.

Separate the crespelle and lay them out on a work surface. Divide the spinach among the crespelle and spread out evenly. Scatter 2 cups/ 225 g of the Toma over the spinach on the crespelle, dividing it evenly. Season with salt and pepper. Fold the crespelle in half, then in half again to form a loose triangle.

Grease the inside of a 6-by-12-in/15-by- 30.5-cm ceramic baking dish with 1 tbsp of the butter. Arrange the filled crespelle in the dish, slightly overlapping.

In a small saucepan, combine the remaining 1 tbsp butter and the cream and heat over medium heat until the cream is simmering all over the surface (not just at the edges of the pan). Remove from the heat, add the Parmigiano, and stir to melt the cheese into the cream. Pour the hot cream mixture over the crespelle and scatter on the remaining ½ cup/55 g Toma cheese.

Bake for 10 to 12 minutes, or until cheese is melted and the edges of the crespelle are crisp. Serve hot.

2½ lb/1.2 kg spinach, large stems removed, well rinsed

10 oz/280 g Toma cheese, shredded

Sea salt and freshly cracked black pepper

2 tbsp unsalted butter

1 cup/240 ml heavy (whipping) cream

¼ cup/30 g freshly grated Parmigiano-Reggiano cheese

SPINACH SPAETZLE WITH CRUCOLO

SERVES 4 TO 6

1 lb/455 g spinach, large stems removed, well rinsed

1½ cups/360 ml whole milk

4 large eggs

3 cups/385 g all-purpose flour

Sea salt

A few gratings of fresh nutmeg

6 tbsp/85 g unsalted butter, at room temperature

8 oz/225 g Crucolo or young Asiago cheese, grated

Crucolo is a raw cow's-milk cheese from the Alto Adige in northern Italy. Similar in texture to Asiago, Crucolo has a much sweeter, tangier buttermilk flavor and is fantastic raw as a table cheese, in a sandwich with salty ham, or melted over risotto, pasta, and especially the typical spinach spaetzle from the same region.

Bring a large pot of water to a boil over high heat. Add the spinach to the boiling water and blanch for 30 seconds. Using tongs or a wire-mesh strainer, plunge the spinach into an ice water bath to stop the cooking. Remove the hot water from the heat and reserve the water to cook the spaetzle in later.

Drain the spinach from the ice water and squeeze with your hands to get out as much water as possible. In a food processor fitted with the blade attachment, combine the spinach and milk and pulse until the spinach is very finely chopped. Add the eggs and pulse just until well blended.

In a large bowl, whisk together the flour, 2 tsp salt, and nutmeg. Add the spinach mixture and stir until well mixed. (You may need to add a touch more flour or milk; you want a sticky batter that is still loose enough to push through the holes of a spaetzle maker.)

Return the spinach-blanching water to a boil over high heat and add a small handful of salt. Have ready an ice water bath.

When the water is boiling, put about ½ cup/ 115 g of the batter in a spaetzle maker or a colander. Using a rubber spatula, push the batter through the holes directly into the boiling water and cook until the spaetzle float and look plump and firm, 1 to 2 minutes. Using a strainer or slotted spoon, plunge the spaetzle into the ice water to stop the cooking, then immediately drain and transfer to a large bowl. Repeat to cook the remaining batter.

(The spaetzle can be made up to this point up to 3 hours ahead. Toss with a little melted butter or a drizzle of extra-virgin olive oil to prevent them from sticking and set aside at room temperature.)

When ready to serve, melt the butter in a large sauté pan or skillet over medium-high heat. Add the spaetzle and sauté, shaking the pan from time to time, allowing little golden spots to appear here and there. Remove from the heat, scatter the cheese over the spaetzle, and stir to combine well. Transfer to a warmed serving dish and serve immediately.

COFFEE-RUBBED LEG OF LAMB STUFFED WITH SPINACH AND AGED CHEDDAR

SERVES 4 TO 6

FOR THE COFFEE RUB:

2 tbsp fresh, finely ground coffee beans

1½ tbsp sea salt

2 tsp freshly cracked black pepper

2 tsp finely chopped fresh rosemary

I had been meaning to try cooking lamb with coffee for years. When the clever lads at Beehive Cheese in Utah developed "Barely Buzzed," their now-famous Cheddar rubbed with ground coffee and lavender, I knew the time had come to experiment.

While I am a big fan of their unique artisanal creation, I find that what makes Barely Buzzed special can get lost when cooked. So I played around a bit with the flavor profiles of really good aged Cheddar and freshly ground coffee set against the full-flavored leg of lamb and wilted spinach. This stunning main dish is the result. Thanks go to Beehive for the inspiration; if you like the combination of coffee and cheese, you need to seek out some Barely Buzzed.

TO MAKE THE RUB: In a small bowl, combine the coffee, salt, pepper, and rosemary and set aside.

Preheat the oven to 425°F/220°C. Fit a wire rack in a large roasting pan.

Soak the spinach leaves in cold water for 5 minutes to loosen any sand, then drain and rinse well. Heat a large sauté pan over high heat. Add the spinach with whatever water is still clinging to the leaves and wilt, using a pair of tongs to help move the spinach around. When the spinach is collapsed, remove from the heat and transfer to a colander to cool to room temperature. Squeeze the cooked and cooled spinach with your hands to release as much water as you can and set aside.

Open up the leg of lamb, laying it on the fat side. Trim any excess fat, and butterfly it by cutting a flap into any areas that rise above an even thickness. Open the flaps flat, like the pages of a book. With the tip of a sharp knife, cut several slits all along the heavier parts of the meat. Season the lamb with salt and pepper and the rosemary, pushing some of the seasoning into the slits. Scatter the spinach evenly over the whole surface, then top with the Cheddar.

Roll the leg of lamb tightly lengthwise like a jelly roll. Using kitchen string, tie the lamb snugly at regular intervals. Rub the olive oil over the lamb, then massage the coffee rub all over and into the meat. Transfer to the rack in the roasting pan and place in the oven. Roast for 30 minutes, then reduce the oven temperature to 350°F/180°C and cook for 35 to 45 minutes longer, or until an instant-read thermometer inserted in the center of the lamb registers 115°F/45°C for rare, or slightly longer for medium.

Remove from the oven, tent with aluminum foil, and let rest for 20 minutes. Remove the string, carve across the grain into thin slices, and serve.

2 lb/910 g spinach, large stems removed

2½ lb/1.2 kg boneless leg of lamb

Sea salt and freshly cracked black pepper

1 tsp finely chopped fresh rosemary

6 oz/170 g good-quality aged Cheddar cheese, grated

2 tbsp extra-virgin olive oil

INDEX